SWINDLERS TRAVERSING THE GLOBE

Swindlers, scammers and confidence tricksters have particular attributes that allow them to succeed (at least for a time) in their pursuit of money or prestige. In general they are clever, talented, plausible, charismatic and often well educated, but lack the discipline to properly apply themselves to long term study or legitimate careers. They love to dress and live well but often fail in business, and the losses incurred by others at their expense do not seem to trouble them.

The narcissists in this Australian study sought to gain or maintain the lifestyle they believed they deserved. Most were the black sheep in good families. Undeserved titles (military, medical or other) were sometimes assumed.

In the 'Sun' (Sydney) on July 27th 1947 the NSW Police Commissioner William Mackay quoted Scotland Yard as saying that the world's leading confidence men were mostly Australians, with a sprinkling of Scots and Americans. With a small population and limited resources at home, some Australians were forced to go abroad to get into the big money.

Matthew Biggar (1881-1948)

Biggar was born at Poowong in Victoria, Australia on July 30th 1881. He was the second youngest of seven children born to farmer Alexander Biggar and Ethel (nee Turner) and seems to be the only criminal member of the family. His parents lived until 1938 and 1934 respectively, so he was not orphaned or left to his own devices at an early age.

Various later newspapers record that Matthew Biggar's first conviction was in 1905 and he served six months for larceny under the name of Henry/Harry Howe. The 'Evening Star' (New Zealand) of October 21st 1915 states that Scotland Yard traced that trial to Walkerston in Queensland (near Mackay) on September 4th 1905. There is no mention in newspapers of the period but Henry Howe is listed in the index of a Queensland Police Gazette in 1906 (probably for his release).

The next known conviction was in New Zealand in August 1909, under the alias of Patrick Dalton. He and a fellow "Australian spieler" in May 1909 had conspired in a railway carriage between Belfast and Christchurch to defraud a traveler using a three-card trick. He had already spent three months in Lyttleton Gaol in Christchurch awaiting trial, and was sentenced to another nine months in prison.

As Robert Wilson (alias Bradshaw, Dalton and Howe) Biggar faced court in Bundaberg Queensland on July 29th 1910. This related to a theft in 1907 at Mount Perry, when Wilson had been released on bail pending trial but failed to appear. He was now arrested in New South Wales and taken to Bundaberg, found guilty of stealing £5 from a person (picking a pocket) and sentenced to two years with hard labour.

Biggar sailed for England and in May 1914 a Bow Street Magistrate found him guilty (as Robert Bradshaw) of loitering with intent to commit a confidence trick after he was arrested in Northumberland Avenue. Later newspapers reported that he served three months in prison and was then liberated on condition that he left England for Canada. He may have traveled to Canada as Robert Henry Bradshaw on 'Calgarian' (as a tourist) and arrived on September 4th 1914.

Matthew Biggar often sailed under his real name, and moved frequently between England, Canada and America. As a "farmer" he arrived in Canada from Liverpool on 'Megantic' on June 6th 1915. By July 14th 1915 he was in a San Francisco gaol as Robert Watson alias "Lord Gordon", one of a trio of swindlers. On July 9th 1915 one of the trio met a New Zealander named James Howell at Cook's Tour Office in the city. The next day Howell met "Lord Gordon", supposedly an Irishman who had recently fallen heir to a huge estate and wished to distribute some money to the poor in New Zealand. The Howell brothers agreed to take care of this task when they returned to New Zealand, and were asked to put up $30,000 as evidence of their good faith in administering the money. They became suspicious and on July 13th 1915 Robert Watson was arrested in Jefferson Square.

Two of the trio (including Biggar alias Watson alias Lord Gordon) were still in gaol in San Francisco in late August 1915, but by September 28th they had absconded. A Judge had given them liberty on a writ of habeas corpus without the knowledge of criminal authorities, and police only learned of the escape twelve hours later. By now San Francisco police had received full details of the criminal histories of the gang from Scotland Yard, after sending over fingerprint records. Apparently Robert Watson was also wanted by Toronto police (the details are unknown).

Later newspapers reported that two months after absconding from San Francisco, Biggar was sentenced to six months prison in Santiago for vagrancy as Robert Mitchell. The sentence was reportedly suspended and he left for Montreal. I cannot find any contemporary references to this affair.

The next we hear of Matthew Biggar is in London in June 1916, when he applied to join the British Army for the war. One wonders why he did not apply to join the Australian Imperial Forces, but there was a suggestion that he actually wanted to join the Royal Air Force so that he could play at cards with the officers, and had returned to London from China for this purpose. He was living in the 'Russell Hotel' in Russell Square, and his occupation is shown as "salesman" with the next of kin his mother in Victoria. Newspapers reported that he deserted from 'King Edward's Horse' and received a military punishment before he was transferred to the 'Rifle Brigade' and sent to France.

On April 12th 1917 Biggar received a severe leg wound resulting in amputation of the left leg above the knee, and he was later described as “one-legged Harry” or “Pegtop Smith”. Requiring crutches or an artificial leg, he was pensioned out of the army on February 13th 1918, but seems to have received the “British War Medal” and the “Victory Medal”. His address after discharge was in Maida Vale in London. In May 1923 his wife (more of that later) was living in Farquar Road Upper Norwood with her mother and trying to obtain proof of her husband’s military discharge from authorities (he was apparently in Belgium).

After the war Matthew Biggar reportedly formed a British gang called the “Scientific Six”, which specialized in sharping wealthy Americans and “colonials” at auction bridge and poker in hotels and hydros. On November 17th 1920 Matthew Biggar (“horse dealer” living at 11 Hay Hill with father Alexander a farmer in Victoria) married Ella Heather Camplisson (nee Clement of the same address with no occupation). Ella was born in Berkshire in October 1893, and married English-born Charles Edward Camplisson (who had earlier emigrated to Canada) while he was on leave in London in August 1915. Camplisson suffered from shell-shock acquired in Ypres in April 1915, then chronic endocarditis from March 1917 and spent the whole war in hospitals. He was discharged in mid February 1918 and payments to Ella (living in Upper Norwood but not with her mother) ceased on March 1st 1918. Camplisson arrived back in Canada on March 16th 1918 and did not die until 1945, so Ella was not a widow as she stated when she married Matthew Biggar in 1920.

On January 3rd 1921 Biggar and other gang members conspired at Hay Hill West to obtain two amounts of £5 from Major Walter Roche at "Anzac Poker". Biggar absconded on bail, leaving two fellow conspirators to face trial at the 'Old Bailey' in March 1921. They were sentenced to two years with hard labour. The "cultured, well-dressed Captain Biggar" allegedly sailed to America, and was not heard of until October 1923 when he fleeced a "colonial" of £100 at cards in an Edinburgh hotel. Police traced Biggar to the 'Great Western Hotel' in Paddington where he was arrested on November 3rd. On November 22nd 1923 at Marlborough Street Police Court he pleaded guilty to the 1921 charge and was sentenced to two consecutive terms of five months for false pretenses. While the defense insisted the accused was named Matthew Biggar, the prosecution believed that his real name was Robert Bradshaw. He supposedly had "a pair of beautiful hands with the supple fingers of a musician, and a keen eye and quickness of brain".

'Truth' (Sydney) on September 30th 1928 stated that earlier in 1923 Robert Bradshaw was convicted in Paris of swindling (with gang members including "Bludger Bill" Warren) and was sentenced to one year in prison (reduced to four months on appeal). He was reportedly bookmaking, which was illegal in France.

While Matthew Biggar probably spent most of 1924 in an English gaol, and pursued his international criminal activities, Ella moved back in with her mother in Farquar Road Upper Norwood. She traveled alone from England to Canada in May 1925 (perhaps chasing her husband?) with her next of kin stated as her mother and a sister, and returned in September 1925. On September 17th 1927 she left London for Melbourne Australia on 'Otranto' and her address was now 12 High View Road Norwood. She stayed in a Melbourne hotel until her return on 'Orvieto', arriving in London on March 29th 1928.

Throughout 1926, 1927 and 1928 Matthew Biggar traveled between Australia and Canada, often purporting to be a "cattle breeder". In July 1928, after a year's searching by Canadian and American police, Biggar was arrested in Victoria British Columbia after arriving in Vancouver on board 'Niagara' from Sydney. He was suspected of swindling a Dutch East Indies visitor (Dr. Otto Bohrsmann) of $31, 486 in Atlantic City in May 1927, through a horse-betting scam involving phone-tapping. Biggar was freed in Canada when American authorities dropped the charges, and by September 1928 he was staying at the 'Hotel Mansions' in Sydney under the name of George Anderson.

Biggar was quickly identified and locked up in the debtor's prison at 'Long Bay Gaol' in Sydney after Dr. Otto Bohrsmann issued a writ of damages for £10,000 owed to him. Biggar now voluntarily declared himself bankrupt. He had been deported from Canada on the grounds that he might be a charge on the State (as a cripple) and he received a very small war pension from England. Any money he received was from work as an advertising agent, a commission from a Cuban bookmaking syndicate and gambling. He had once been a salesman in China. He was aware that his wife had recently left Australia to return to her mother. He was declared bankrupt on October 12th 1928 and released from prison.

Matthew Biggar continued to travel the world. On January 17th 1929 he returned to London from Brisbane and his address was once again the 'Russell Hotel' in Russell Square. In May 1930 in London as Algernon Adams he and an accomplice swindled a New Zealander named George Sexton out of £10,000 through a "secret racing syndicate". According to the authors of a book 'Gangland Australia' published in 2014, in 1935 Biggar defrauded a South African named Daniel de Wet for £9.900. Biggar was probably a passenger from England to Cape Town in September 1937, with his occupation listed as "estate agent". In the 1939 UK census Ella Biggar (now back to Clement but probably not divorced) was living with her mother in Bromley in Kent as an unpaid domestic servant. Also in the household lived Edward Ernest Ironside (a van driver and mechanic), and Ella and Ironside married later that year (she used her maiden name of Clement). Ella probably died in Kent in mid-1957.

As Matthew Henderson alias John Freeman, commission agent, Biggar was found guilty of conspiracy to defraud at London's 'Old Bailey' in June 1944. In league with Australian swindler Gerald Riviere, Biggar defrauded a retired cotton manufacturer of £1,800 in a horse-racing betting scam. Also found guilty of stealing £50 from another man by pretending the money would be invested in bloodstock, Henderson was sentenced to a total of three years imprisonment.

On January 22nd 1948 Matthew Henderson of no fixed abode died in hospital at Kingston Upon Thames in London. The "elderly, one-legged man with threadbare but immaculately cut clothes" and no identification papers had collapsed on a London bus. When his name was released, Detective-Inspector Jock Horrocks went to the Kensington mortuary and immediately identified him as Matthew Biggar, the "most notorious confidence man on the records". Scotland Yard was able to confirm this using fingerprint records. In his heyday Biggar had allegedly earned half of a £95,000 haul by his gang in one year, and had driven a £2,000 Rolls Royce and enjoyed the finest wines and cigars. Horrocks collected from his colleagues in the force to pay for Biggar's funeral expenses. He was taken to the Kingston Cemetery (in a Rolls Royce hearse according to the 'Daily Telegraph' of Sydney) and buried as Matthew Henderson on January 26th 1948.

Matthew Biggar alias Algernon Adams May 1930

Matthew Biggar alias George Anderson 1928

Sketch of Matthew Biggar 1948

Arthur Guy Carless (1886-1955)

Arthur was the son of a Hereford solicitor who served as the Hereford Town Clerk for forty one years. He was born in Hereford on October 3rd 1886 and was educated at Hereford Cathedral School and Clifton College in Bristol. Destined for the Bar like his father and older brother, Arthur failed his exams.

When Arthur's father died in 1909, he left property from which Arthur received £170 per year. In the census of 1911 he was staying at the 'Inns of Court Hotel' at High Holborn and his occupation showed that he was of independent means. In that year he made two quick trips to New Zealand, and in 1913 he was living in Auckland and working as a tobacconist. In 1914 he was in Timaru and then Oamaru as a billiard saloon proprietor. On August 19th 1914 he was fined £5 at Oamaru for obscene language. He was described as 5'10" in height with auburn hair, blue eyes, a medium build and a blotched face. In December 1914 he did not defend two small civil suits in the Magistrate's Court at Oamaru.

On August 16th 1915 Arthur Guy Carless arrived in Sydney from New Zealand on 'Moeraki'. In May 1916 he was living in Mosman in Sydney and was the proprietor of a tobacco and hairdressing shop on the same premises. He was fined at North Sydney Police Court for knowingly and wilfully allowing the shop to be used for betting purposes, having pleaded guilty. On June 30th 1916 he arrived in Vancouver Canada from Sydney on 'Niagara'. The manifest stated that he had last been in

Canada in 1911 (for two weeks) and that his occupation was "tobacconist". On July 17th 1916 he arrived in England from Montreal on 'Grampian'. There was no occupation listed and his last permanent residence was in Australia.

In January 1917 Arthur Guy Carless married Katherine Rosamond Lord at Hammersmith in London. In 1918 their address was "Rose Cottage" in Stepney London, but by June 1918 Arthur had left his wife. Katherine Carless died at Kensington on November 4th 1930, leaving the administration of her estate of £452 2s to Arthur's spinster sister Henrietta Mary Carless. Katherine's last residence was listed as "Rosslyn House" Twickenham Park.

The 'Western Daily Press' of July 27th 1925 reported that in 1918 Arthur obtained a position with a £400 per year salary and was sent to Shanghai, but left the job and went to America. On June 20th 1918 he arrived in Seattle Washington on 'Kamo Maru' from London and his home address was now in his hometown of Hereford. He was an "auctioneer" by occupation. In the 1919 Seattle directory he was listed as proprietor of the 'Reliable Investment Company'. The 'Western Daily Express' (mentioned above) reported that in 1919 Carless opened up a business in America with another man and they disappeared when they were in trouble for fraudulently obtaining money from four men by advertising for a business manager with capital. They were reportedly arrested in Montreal but made restitution and the charges were dropped.

On November 12th 1920 A.G. Carless and another man named Finch were arrested in Cleveland Ohio, charged with false pretenses (Carless was also charged with conspiracy to defraud). They had sold an interest in the 'Instantaneous Liquid Heater Company" to a Pittsburgh woman for $500 but there was no such device and the company was organized by the men to victimise investors. I cannot find any further reference to the matter so presumably restitution was again made and charges dropped.

Sometime during this period Arthur Guy Carless met Candian-born widow Louise Gertrude Vickers. After her husband died in Canada in 1917, Louise and her son John Henry Vickers went to live in Birmingham, England. Her husband had been a building contractor working in both England and Vancouver. Although not married (Katherine Rosamond was still alive) Louise and Arthur lived as man and wife during the 1920's and a son Joseph Ronald Carless was born (supposedly on May 14th 1921 in Vancouver although I cannot find a birth record). Ronald was administrator of his mother's estate when she died in Oswestry in 1963 (she had remarried and Ronald was a motor body paint sprayer). Although he informally used the surname "Carless" while Arthur was around, John Henry Vickers died in France as "Vickers" in October 1939 and is buried there in 'Choloy War Cemetery'.

On January 8th 1922 the 'Maheno' arrived in Sydney Australia carrying Arthur Carless and his "wife" as well as a child named Jack. There was no listing for baby

Ronald. The 'Advertiser' (Adelaide) of January 13th 1922 reported upon a lost child in Melbourne. Jack Carless aged 6½ had been found wandering around Bourke Street. He believed that he was born in England. He and his parents had arrived in Sydney on 'Maheno' and caught the train to Melbourne. They were staying in apartments opposite a park, and he had exited from a wrong gate at the park and become lost. He said he had lived in America for the last two years. His parents came to the Russell Street Police Station looking for him and all was well.

Arthur Carless did not remain in Melbourne. In 1922 in Adelaide he formed a company called 'Standard Securities' and with another criminal named Abe Ash (Belltopper Jim) ran the 'Commercial Traders' Investment Company'. They advertised for partners and relieved prospective partners of their cash, but apparently Abe pocketed most of the money and swindled his co-conspirator. Detectives became inquisitive and hoped to intercept Carless at Port Adelaide before he escaped, but were too late.

On March 12th 1923 Arthur Carless, his "wife" Louise and sons Jack (aged 7) and Ronald (aged 2) arrived in London from Adelaide on 'Balranald'. He was an auctioneer and his contact address was c/- 'Carless and Capel' solicitors in Hereford (his old family firm).

In May 1925 Arthur Guy Carless (auctioneer of Hall Green Birmingham) was charged in Birmingham England with conspiring to defraud. He was managing director of business broker ‘Commercial Exchange Ltd' and between June and December 1924 had advertised for works managers for 'Domino Ltd’ and ‘Unite Ltd’. Several men were defrauded through investing in these companies. At the ‘Birmingham Assizes' on July 24th 1925 he was found guilty of conspiracy with a manufacturer (owner of the two companies) to obtain money by false representations. He was sentenced to 18 months prison. and since his return to England in March 1923 many complaints had been received in Birmingham about his transactions.

Probably this gaol term severed ties between Arthur Carless and Louise Gertrude Vickers (nee Murphy). Family researchers state that in January 1928 in Belfast Northern Ireland a daughter named Sheila Diane Carless was born to Arthur and the much younger Mary Constance Smart. After Katherine Rosamond Carless died in November 1930, Arthur and Mary Constance were free to marry, and they did so in Rathdown Ireland in December 1931.

In November 1928 Arthur Guy Carless was a “business transfer agent” for the firm ‘Northern Agency’ (also an auctioneer) and was living at "Lyndhurst", Alexandra Mount, Litherland in Lancashire. On November 29th he appeared at Liverpool Police Court with three other men on a charge of conspiracy. The scam was the same – false representations were made that there was a business or a partnership in a genuine business to be bought. Either the business did not exist or its prosperity was misrepresented. On February 14th sentencing at Liverpool was postponed for more charges to be brought and the trial was transferred to the Manchester Assizes, where on February 26th 1929 Carless was sentenced to three years imprisonment for fraudulent conversion, fraud and conspiracy. He was released on license from 'Parkhurst Prison' on July 6th 1931. The UK 'Register of Habitual Criminals' in 1929 recorded interesting details about Carless. He was well-educated, very plausible, very clever, he walked with a swinging gait, spoke with a slight American accent, always carried a walking stick, was an inveterate whiskey drinker and cigarette smoker, had a strong personality, was fond of women of ill-repute, had traveled all over the world and was in receipt of an annual income from his father's estate (his mother had died in 1920 so the income may have increased).

The 'Belfast Telegraph' of October 17th 1934 tells us that after his release in July 1931, Carless went to Ireland and opened up another employment business in the name of 'Smart & Co.'. He was arrested in Dublin and accused of false pretenses but was acquitted at the 'Dublin Circuit Court'.

A son Joseph Donald Carless was born to Arthur and Mary Constance Carless in London on March 29th 1934. From at least 1933 until 1936 the family were living in Elmstead Avenue Wembley in London. After leaving Dublin, Arthur had gone to London and opened up the business of 'Reynolds & Co'. In May 1934 he appeared before the Marlborough Street Police Court as one of several men charged with conspiracy to defraud and false pretenses in connection with shares in a company called

‘Trade Competitions Ltd.’. Yet again, the fraud related to employment and underwriting. At the 'Old Bailey' on October 16th 1934 the “business transfer agent” was sentenced to five years imprisonment. In December 1934 the ‘Court of Criminal Appeal' quashed the conviction on the grounds that the indictment (which contained many counts) was badly drawn, and that the ‘Common Serjeant’ had misdirected the jury. Carless had been unwell, spending seven weeks in the hospital at Wandsworth Gaol, and he fainted in the dock after the decision.

In June 1936 Carless sued ‘Truth’ (UK) for libel over an article published on October 17th 1934 that exposed his crooked dealings. Mention was made of similar frauds committed by Carless in the United States, Canada and Australia (some of them in partnership with a man who was convicted with him at Liverpool in 1929). ‘Truth' warned of fraud relating to 'Reynolds & Co.' and 'Hannan Staples & Co.'. A special jury in the ‘King’s Bench Division' stopped the libel action and added that the publishers had "done a public service" in exposing Carless. All his frauds worked along similar lines - advertisements invited applications from traders and others requiring capital for the acquisition or development of a business, and their victims were diddled out of fees and commissions for which they got no return except perhaps a useless skeleton of a company without any cash.

After 1936 Arthur Guy Carless remained largely out of the newspapers. In the 1939 UK census he was living at

“The Knoll” in Ross and Whitechurch, Herefordshire with Mary Constance and young Joseph Donald. His occupation was given as "commercial traveller". In March 1945 he was living in Edgbaston Birmingham when he was fined £10 for cruelly sending four Irish setter puppies in a tea chest from Birmingham to Grantham. They had to be put down.

Sheila Diane Carless married in Birmingham Warwickshire in 1949. Joseph Ronald Carless married in Solihull Warwickshire in 1949. From at least 1945 Arthur and Mary were living at Edgbaston in Birmingham. Arthur died in Hastings Sussex on August 16th 1955, while Mary was still living in Edgbaston until 1957. She died on May 5th 1983 and was then living at Harborne in Birmingham. Her estate was a massive £74,486, which indicates to me that Arthur had managed to squirrel away much of his ill-gotten gains.

Despite his years of notoriety, I am unable to find a photo or illustration of Arthur Guy Carless, but below are photos of his children Joseph Ronald, Sheila and Joseph Donald and his wife Mary Constance.

Joseph Ronald Carless

Joseph Donald Carless

Mary Constance & Sheila Carless

Charles Ernest Chadwick (c.1870-1952)

This elusive character was possibly the world's greatest bigamist as he swindled his way throughout the globe using a multitude of names.

Using the earliest available Australian newspaper articles and official records, we can pin his origins down to a certain extent. Chadwick's New South Wales gaol record from 1893 lists two earlier criminal convictions. At Newtown Police Court in Sydney on July 1st 1889 Charles Ernest Chadwick (aged seventeen with no occupation, making him born in 1872) was found guilty of stealing money from the 'General Gordon Hotel' at Marrickville, where his mother worked. He was sentenced to two months with hard labour. At the Wollongong Police Court (south of Sydney) on October 30th 1890 he was sentenced to three months with hard labour for false pretenses (uttering a valueless cheque). At the time he was living in a Wollongong boarding house and suffering from illness and fainting fits due to palpitation of the heart.

From April 3rd 1891 Chadwick was in Darlinghurst Gaol awaiting trial for forgery and was under medical examination there. Initially he was in a very weak state and suffered from a delusion that he was to inherit a large sum of money. The documents forged purported to be letters of administration and the will of a deceased friend, and through them he obtained a little money from the family with whom he was lodging at Redfern on March 17th. Chadwick (a clerk) was nineteen years of age (again putting his birth at around 1872). At trial on July 1st 1891 the judge declared that the jury acquit the accused of forgery (he probably should have been charged with false pretences) since the documents "contained a lot of nonsense that might have been the outcome of a disordered brain".

On October 15th 1891 Charles Ernest Chadwick married Frances Mary Skelly at Windsor west of Sydney. Her first child May Gwendoline Skelly had been born at Wisemans Ferry on October 10th 1890 (with no father listed). On the 1891 marriage certificate Charles is shown as a "labourer". There is no information about birthplaces, parents or ages. At Yass in July 1893 Frances testified that prior to the marriage she had worked for three years as a nurse at Windsor Hospital, while Charles worked as a wardsman there for eighteen months. At Liverpool in Sydney in 1892 daughter Mary Ellen Chadwick was born.

The next mention of Charles Ernest Chadwick in newspapers is in June 1893, when he was posing as a doctor at Gunning in country New South Wales. On three occasions in May he had fraudulently obtained a total of £36 from his neighbour in Gunning (a tailor) by falsely representing that Marion Chadwick now agreed (after he won his case in court) that he was entitled to some of his father's estate and that he was about to receive £1,000. The 'Goulburn Evening Post' of July 8th 1893 gives very useful detail about evidence given at the trial at Yass on July 4th. Frances Mary Chadwick testified about their time at Windsor (as mentioned above) and the two children. They had come to Gunning from Canley Vale. To the best of her belief her husband had a medical education in England, and he had practiced for a short time in Sydney. Her husband was the sole support of herself and children (there was a little furniture but nothing to live upon).

It is the deposition of Charles Ernest Chadwick at the Yass Quarter Sessions on July 4th 1893 that gives us clues to his ancestry. Much of what he says is rambling, contradictory and fanciful, but some is correct. He says his age is twenty-seven (probably incorrect) and that he was born in Sheffield England. He says his father William Chadwick had died intestate prior to 1889, leaving some money and land at Canterbury in Sydney. He calls the widow variously "Mrs. Chadwick”, “the widow” and “my mother”. This woman had sworn that there was no issue from the marriage (so she was not his biological mother) and she did not want Charles to inherit any of the estate. William Charles Chadwick had died at the ‘Woolpack Hotel' in Canterbury on December 11th 1886, reportedly at the age of sixty-four. He was supposedly from England, and was a wood carter by occupation.

Various family researchers state that William Charles Chadwick and Marion Black were the parents of Charles Ernest Chadwick. Since this information was not on the copy of the marriage certificate that I have, it may have been in the divorce records of 1898. William Charles Chadwick (bachelor with no birthplace, parental details or age) married Marion Blackwell (spinster and no parental, birthplace or age information) married in Sydney on 23rd March 1869. William was a "farmer" living in York Street and Marion was a dressmaker living in Palmer Street. I believe that these are the individuals who parented Charles Ernest Chadwick, who was probably born in Sydney after the marriage and may have been the illegitimate son of William.

After the death of William Charles Chadwick in December 1886, Marion had to fight for probate of the estate, and this was finally granted in January 1893. Throughout this period Mrs. Chadwick was living at Canterbury New Road in Marrickville, and then she disappears from records. This battle over the estate surely explains the obsession of Charles with inheritance and his unfair impoverishment.

At the Yass Quarter Sessions on July 4th 1893, Charles deposed that his father sent him back to England in 1886, that he had returned in 1889 and had attended medical college at Oxford University. I don't believe any of this, but somehow he managed over the years to represent himself successfully as a medical doctor. The jury found him guilty of fraudulently obtaining the £36 and he was sentenced to 18 months in Goulburn Gaol.

In Sydney in August 1898 Frances Mary Chadwick (nee Skelly) petitioned for divorce on the grounds of desertion, and the marriage was dissolved on December 6th 1898 with Frances retaining custody of Mary Ellen. Frances had not seen Charles since 1894. After his release from prison on the Gunning charge they lived in several places and at Coolamon he was again sentenced to three months in prison for false pretences. He was discharged on February 27th 1895.

In August 1895 a warrant was issued at Redfern in Sydney for the arrest of Henry Westwood Cooper (believed to be identical with Charles Ernest Chadwick) who had signed a certificate as a medical practitioner on May 13th (not being such). I am unable to find any further reference to this alleged offence. On June 17th 1895 at Redfern Henry Westwood Irving Llewellyn Cooper married teenager Helen Scott (she believed he was a physician).

Now adopting the new name, "Cooper" was by April 1896 fraudulently practicing as a doctor at Pittsworth in Queensland. Presumably he had already abandoned Helen (there were no children from that marriage). He declared that he had practiced in New Zealand using an American diploma. At Toowoomba Police Court on May 14th 1896 he was fined. On June 12th 1896 in Brisbane he married teenager Bertha Ethel Young as Henry Irwin Llewellyn Cooper.

On August 2nd 1896 "Cooper" and Bertha left Australia for England "to claim the Chadwick estates" and on November 9th 1896 they moved on to America. Several newspapers in 1912 state that in December 1896 Cooper was in trouble in Philadelphia for depositing a worthless draft but I cannot find any contemporary accounts to back up this assertion. Before they left Australia, "Cooper" reportedly swindled Bertha's wealthy aunt

Mrs. MacDonald in Melbourne of £500 (which he "borrowed"). By June 4th 1897 Toronto police were looking for "forger, quack and probable bigamist" Henry Westwood Cooper. He had worked at Toronto General Hospital and eloped with teenager Ida Maud Campaign to Shelburne (they married in Toronto on May 24th 1897). In Shelburne he reportedly secured $100 from "trusting parties" during his brief stay. Bertha was abandoned in Toronto and her mother hurried over to rescue her. By September 1901 they were living in Buffalo New York and were able to testify at a trial in San Francisco. There were no children from the marriages with Bertha or Ida.

In June 1897 Cooper fleeced his Chicago landlady Mrs. Mary Murphy out of $1,400 using a worthless draft on the Bank of New South Wales. He moved on to the 'Langhorn Hotel' in San Francisco and added the title "Sir" to his name. He reportedly made plans to elope with a married but separated waitress named Fanning, who was in court to support him in August 1897 (along with Ida who was staying with Mrs. Fanning). Sir Henry was charged with depositing a worthless draft for £150 sterling on the Bank of New South Wales at the Crocker-Woolworth National Bank. Still obsessed with his failure to inherit, he forged letters purporting to show that he had been left money by an aunt. He was arrested on August 31st 1897 but the trial was postponed after he suffered a hemorrhage of the lungs in gaol. By November his real identity was known through police in Sydney. On December 6th 1897 Sir Harry was found guilty of uttering and passing a fictitious cheque, and on December 21st he was sentenced to three years in San Quentin prison. Ida returned to her family in Toronto. On December 4th 1900 in Sydney, Helen Scott (unaware of his first marriage as Chadwick, which made her 1895 marriage bigamous) filed for divorce from Cooper.

On January 15th 1901 Sir Harry Westwood Cooper was released from San Quentin Prison. In March 1899 he had been involved in a plot to murder guards and escape. When the plot was discovered he turned informer, and spent more than a year in an “incorrigible cell”. By February 1901 Sir Harry was in Crockett California, where he worked for about a week as a waiter at the 'Star Hotel'. Then as Ernest Moore Chadwick, licensed physician in New Zealand, he received thousands of dollars in credit and swindled various merchants in the town. Again he said that he had just received word that he had been left a large sum of money by a rich aunt in London, forging a telegram to that effect. Staying at Daniel Schneider’s hotel in Vallejo Junction, he eloped with a teenage daughter Norine Pearl Schneider and married her at Crockett on Saturday February 23rd 1901 as Sir Harry Westwood Cooper. He had forged a telegram supposedly from her mother, consenting to the marriage.

Having left by train, the couple arrived at Ogden in Utah and on February 28th 1901 Sir Harry Westwood Cooper alias Dr. Ernest Moore Chadwick was arrested on charges of forgery and bigamy. Norine was anxious to return home. After a trial in June at which the jury could not agree, in San Francisco on October 5th 1901 Sir Harry was sentenced to ten years prison at San Quentin for forging the Schneider telegram. His Australian "wife" Bertha and her mother testified at the second trial in support of Norine Schneider on September 25th.

In the San Francisco County Gaol on Monday April 6th 1903 a young widow named Theresa May Van Valden (nee Strowbridge) married Ernest Moore Chadwick. A religious enthusiast, she visited the gaol for a Salvation Army gospel mission and fell in love with the inmate.

On September 1st 1911 Cooper/Chadwick was released from San Quentin on parole. He made his way to Oakland California where he set up a medical practice as Dr. Milton Abraham. He presented a worthless bank draft on the Bank of New Zealand, and on February 9th 1912 married nurse Anna Milbraith and secured a loan of $1,000 from her mother before fleeing from Oakland on February 14th. Prior to this he had tried to persuade nurse Daisy Climm to marry him.

On the run, Cooper/Chadwick/Abraham was traced to Halifax in Canada and London. He abandoned Anna in April 1912 in London, after being recognized by an American at a social function, and sailed for Cape Town in South Africa. She wrote to her brother in Indiana asking for passage money home. By July 1912 she was nursing in Chicago and received an inheritance from a maternal aunt in Germany that enabled her to repay her mother.

After abandoning Anna in England, Chadwick (as Norman Ebenezer McKay) deposited four forged certificates on the Bank of New South Wales in Durban South Africa and received $5,000. He moved on to Melbourne and then Sydney on 'Miltiades' in June 1912. On board he was known as "Surgeon-Major Swinton Holme". Authorities suspected that this character might illegally practice as a medical man in New South Wales, and traced him to the town of Burraga near Bathurst. He was working as Dr. James Boyd and had become engaged to a local girl. He was taken to police headquarters in Sydney by a constable on August 3rd 1912, and was immediately identified as the notorious swindler and bigamist of four continents.

American authorities were anxious to have him back in Oakland to be tried for obtaining money under false pretenses, forgery and bigamy, but first he would be sent back to Durban for trial. He left on the steamer 'Marathon' on Saturday December 21st 1912. At the Durban General Sessions in March 1913 Norman Ebenezer McKay pleaded guilty to forgery and was sentenced to 18 months in prison.

In late May 1914 Chadwick was being held in Durban awaiting the arrival of a detective from Oakland to take him back to California for trial. On May 26th 1914 the District Attorney announced that Alameda County authorities would not proceed with the costly extradition, and Chadwick was released in Durban. He started a maternity home at Belgravia near Johannesburg and on July 1st 1914 as Dr. Andrew John Gibson he married

Elizabeth Ethel (Essie) Stafford (a Queensland girl who was a nurse at the hospital).

On April 5th Gibson and his wife left Johannesburg, arriving in Sydney on 'Ionic' and renting a furnished house at Coogee. Police noticed his unsatisfactory business dealings, and "from information received" and with photos of the swindler Chadwick in their possession they arrested him on August 21st. By mid April 1915 a warrant had been issued for the arrest of Dr. Andrew John Gibson (alias etc) at Johannesburg. He was charged with extensive bank frauds and forgery. At Central Police Court in Sydney Australia on August 23rd 1915 he was presented on these two charges, and described as having "the appearance of a prosperous businessman". He was granted hefty bail, and returned to prison awaiting extradition on November 3rd 1915. His daughter to Essie Stafford (Belvia Ethel Gibson) was born at Woollahra in Sydney on October 30th 1915. Essie (nee Stafford) remained in Sydney with Belvia until her death (still as Gibson) in 1974.

In January 1916 Chadwick left Sydney under escort for Johannesburg. On October 18th 1916 he was sentenced to life in prison for bank frauds totaling £3,765. The "life" sentence turned out to be indeterminate, and in October 1924 he was released and returned to Australia. In January 1925 he arrived in England.

At Hants Assizes in November 1925 as Andrew John Gibson he was sentenced to seven years prison for forgery. On May 29th 1925 at Bournemouth he had forged a Treasury warrant voucher on the South Australian government (representing himself as a doctor appointed to examine intending emigrants for the Australian Emigration Scheme) and he also obtained money from Lloyds Bank by false pretences. In July 1932 at Liverpool he married Miss Annie Gladys Tilston under the name Dr. Harry Cecil Darling (Harry Cecil Rutherford Darling was a genuine Macquarie Street specialist in Sydney).

At Bristol in November 1932 Chadwick (as Andrew John Gibson) was sentenced to four years prison for fraud (in September and October he posed as the Government Medical Officer for Kenya and had obtained money from a university graduate who thought he was applying for a position as Chief Chemist in the Kenyan Department of Mines).

Chadwick left prison on November 6th 1935, went to Liverpool and worked as a post office sorter, labourer and herbal shop manager under the name Andrew John Gibson. In May 1936 he was fined as Harry Cecil Darling for assuming the title Doctor of Medicine on April 6th. In July 1936 as Harry Cecil Darling he set up business in County Road Liverpool as a medical herbalist.

On August 3rd 1937 in Liverpool as Andrew John Gibson, Chadwick forged a document purporting to be a Certificate of Probate (supposedly relating to the death of his daughter Nellie Poriotte, who was not dead) from the Supreme Court of Sydney. He obtained money from a bank manager at Walton using the forged certificate on August 5th. On August 14th 1937 Gibson/Chadwick left Liverpool and was found in January 1938 at Smethwick in Birmingham where he was again operating as a medical herbalist. In February 1938 Chadwick (as Andrew John Gibson) was sentenced to 12 months in prison at Liverpool.

Mary Ellen (Nellie) Chadwick (born 1892) had married Walter Thomas Poriotte (the spelling of the surname varies in records) in Sydney in 1912. Walter died in 1936, Nellie remarried in 1942 and died in 1960. Another daughter of Charles Ernest Chadwick (Belvia Gibson born in Sydney in 1915) married the nephew of Walter Thomas Poriotte (John Colman Poriotte) in Sydney in 1942. Charles Ernest Chadwick was to use the Poriotte name when he died (more of that later). Chadwick's first and only legal wife Frances Mary Skelly was reportedly livid with her daughter Nellie for her friendship with his later "wife" Essie Stafford and her daughter Belvia Gibson. Even though she had remarried in 1900, Frances disowned Nellie and left her entire estate when she died in January 1947 to her first daughter May Gwendoline Downey (nee Chadwick).

Around 10pm on December 20th 1939 pregnant Gladys Higginbottom was admitted as a patient to the Stoke-On-Trent City Maternity Hospital in England, suffering bleeding prior to the birth of her fourth child. The locum resident medical officer administered inappropriate drugs and at midnight he performed a small surgical operation on her to check the haemorrhage. At 1.45am on

December 21st she died of heart failure due to ante-partum haemorrhage (before labour and the birth of the baby).

On February 13th 1940 Andrew John Gibson (the authorities thought this was his real name) of Ullet Road Liverpool stood before a stipendiary magistrate on manslaughter charges. Annie (nee Tilston) was still living with him there in 1939 and 1940.

As Harry Cecil Rutherford Darling, Chadwick/Gibson had obtained a position as locum resident medical officer at the Stoke-On-Trent hospital from November 24th 1939 until December 23rd 1939. There were other charges against him in addition to the Higginbottom case from this period. At the Staffordshire Assizes on July 11th 1940 Andrew John Gibson was found guilty of the manslaughter by negligence of Mrs. Higginbottom. After this he pleaded guilty to the other charges and was sentenced to serve three years on each of those eleven charges concurrently with the manslaughter sentence, which was ten years in prison. At this trial Chadwick made no mention of his supposed studying medicine at Oxford in England from 1886 to 1889. This time he said he studied medicine in New South Wales for around 36 months, but did not take a final degree.

In British electoral registers for 1945 Annie G. Darling was living at 63 Stonor Road in Birmingham. Harry C.R. Darling showed at 14 Ullet Road in Liverpool but he was probably still in prison. Australian newspapers in 1950 reported that he was released from prison in 1946. The

Bathurst 'National Advocate' of May 26th 1950 stated that he had last been seen by police some three years prior when following his release from prison he was reported to be in Birmingham.

On March 11th 1948 a petition for divorce from Elizabeth Ethel Gibson (nee Stafford) was delivered to Gibson/Chadwick at 17A Steelhouse Lane Birmingham. When the divorce was completed on October 14th 1949 the notice was delivered to the respondent Dr. H.C. Darling c/- Becketts, Wharfdale Road, Tysley, Birmingham.

On August 5th 1949 Mr. H.C.R. Darling (dry cleaner living at 63 Stonor Road Birmingham) set sail from London on 'Orion' bound for Sydney. On March 29th 1950 he was appointed as medical superintendent of the Sofala District Hospital in country New South Wales Australia, as Dr. Harry Cecil Darling. He disappeared on May 12th 1950 after detectives queried his credentials. Sofala locals reported that his wife from Liverpool had joined him when he was living nearby at Wattle Flat. On January 5th 1950 Anne G. Darling of 63 Stonor Road Birmingham left London on 'Strathnaver' bound for Sydney (her eventual destination was shown on the ship's manifest as Wattle Flat New South Wales and her occupation was shown as "manageress"). On February 29th 1952 Mrs. A. Darling "manageress" of Birmingham arrived back in Southampton in England on 'Orcades', having embarked in Sydney. Anne Gladys Darling (nee Tilston) died in Liverpool England in October 1974.

Newspapers in 1954 trace Chadwick's movements after he left Sofala in May 1950. He worked for a short period as a male nurse at a leper's station on Peel Island near Brisbane in Queensland. Here he met his last "wife" elderly spinster Eliza (Bessie) O'Leary who was born in Brisbane on June 26th 1879. When Chadwick died as Walter Thomas Porriott (an Englishman out in Australia for his health) on August 29th 1952 in Brisbane, he had reportedly been married for little more than a year, and had swallowed up Bessie's life savings. She handed them to him to pay stamp duty on a mythical fortune coming from England (he forged documents from the English Probate Register).

On the Queensland death record for "Porriott" the parents listed were those of the real Walter Thomas Poriotte who had married Nellie Chadwick in 1912. Bessie died on June 26th 1957 and was placed in the same grave as her "husband" at Toowong Cemetery. The O'Leary family (who understandably detested her bogus husband) inscribed on the headstone "BESSIE" DIED 25th JUNE 1957 AND HER HUSBAND (with no name or dates).

I have counted ten marriages and at least two daughters (Nellie Chadwick and Belvia Gibson). How did Charles Ernest Chadwick manage to fool so many respectable and intelligent women and men over the years? He was only short (around 5'7") and not particularly handsome but wherever he went he was popular. He was slim, well-dressed and well-spoken and aged well.

Charles Ernest Chadwick Goulburn NSW 1893

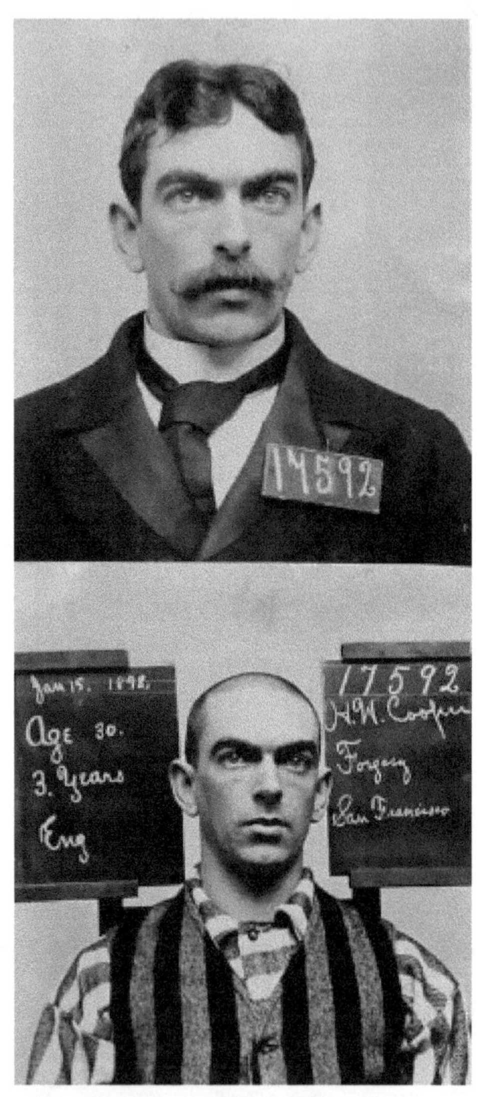

Harry Westwood Cooper San Francisco 1898

Dr. Milton Abraham Oakland California 1912

Dr. Ebenezer McKay or Andrew John Gibson 1915

Dr. Darling/Gibson Sofala NSW 1950

John Joseph Coghlan (1875-1940)

I am convinced that this man was identical with the confidence trickster later known as John James Coghlan, Maudsleigh/Maudsley John Dudley, Joseph Palmer, John Egerton and other aliases, and I trust that the evidence shown here will leave little room for doubt.

Irish immigrant John Francis Coghlan married Josephine Therese Murphy in Sydney Australia in 1874. When John Francis died in 1896 newspapers note that he left a widow and seven children in poor financial circumstances. The births of these seven children were all announced in newspapers as they occurred, but I can only find birth registrations for two of these surviving children. I believe that John Joseph Coghlan was the first-born son announced with a birth date of November 12th 1875. He certainly was the one organising his father's funeral in 1896.

Two Australian newspapers in January 1921 report that Maudsleigh Dudley was born in Sydney and educated at 'Riverview College'. In October 1934 a Catholic journal looking back in history noted that John J. Coghlan had attended 'St. Ignatius College Riverview'. The 'Western Mail' (Perth) of May 9th 1919 reported that Maudsleigh Dudley (the popular son and lyric writer) was a member of a well-known New South Wales family and had lived in Sydney. In March 1895 John J. Coghlan of Sydney had composed a song that was being performed at the 'Tivoli Theatre'.

Although John Francis Coghlan had left his family in a poor financial state, he was once wealthy and a prominent member of society in Sydney. He had made money in the Victorian goldfields in the 1850's and in 1878 in Sydney he formed the 'Australian Diamond Rock Drill and Boring Company Limited'. From December 1882 until 1889 he owned a mansion known as 'Shubra Hall' in Croydon. Despite some business successes, in 1889 he was declared insolvent and had to sell his residence at Croydon, and moved his family to Glebe Point where they lived when he died in July 1896.

It is not surprising that the family reversal of fortunes might have adversely impacted upon the eldest son, particularly after his father's death. Initially as John James Coghlan, by May 1897 he had turned to crime.

The first listed conviction for John James Coghlan was at the Sydney Quarter Sessions on May 28th 1897. He was sentenced to two years with hard labour for stealing and selling eight bicycles using false pretenses between March 3rd and March 11th. In various prison records Coghlan stated that he was born in Sydney, London and New Zealand. He may have been trying to protect his mother and siblings by changing his name and origin. He was a clerk by occupation, 5'8¾" in height with grey eyes, and a mole or wart on the left cheek was often mentioned.

In Hobart Tasmania on May 16th 1899 as John Vasto Cranston (but identified as the same John James Coghlan above), he was sentenced to six months for conspiracy with another man to defraud a victim of £11 in a confidence trick. Back in Sydney, on December 12th 1899 he was sentenced to six months with hard labour for stealing luggage from a train at Redfern Railway Station (in company with another man).

At Melbourne General Sessions on December 3rd 1900 he was sentenced as John Massey Palmer (from 'Rosemont Hall' in Norwood England) to twelve months with hard labour for larceny by a trick. In court he admitted that he was identical to the man convicted in 1897 and 1899. The latest fraud was committed by means of a game played with ten pieces of paper.

On November 13th 1902 at Brisbane Supreme Court John James Coghlan alias Jack Palmer (known locally as "Flash Jack") was sentenced to three years with hard labour for perpetrating a confidence trick in concert with another man. They had allegedly drugged their victim while drinking together in Brisbane on August 6th 1902. They put him on board the 'SS Leura' bound for Sydney, where he awoke to find his money gone. In court Coghlan said they did not drug the victim but induced him to sign a valueless cheque and then threatened him until he went away.

A man identified as John **Joseph** Coghlan was wanted in connection with a confidence trick perpetrated on a German seaman in 'Lloyd's Hotel' in Sydney on May 24th 1905. He was of a similar age and height to the abovementioned criminal, but appears to have eluded apprehension. He probably left Australia soon after this event, but the name he used from this point on soon changed.

In early 1906 John Joseph Coghlan (now Maudsleigh John C. Dudley) married Philippa Victoria Ellis at Southampton in Hampshire. Daughter Estelle Eileen was born in 1907 and son Leslie Clarence in 1908, and for the 1911 census "Coghlan Dudley" and family were living at 59 Lissenden Mansions Highgate Road St Pancras in London. His occupation was "private means" and there were two servants in the household. He was still writing songs and sketches, and in June 1912 the 'Allhambra Music Hall' refused to allow ballet mistress Elise Clerc to perform a sketch of his. The dialogue of the sketch was then held by the High Court to be objectionable. In January 1912 four-year-old Estelle and three-year-old Leslie were photographed for the 'Luton Reporter' as students of Elise Clerc.

In August 1913 "dramatic author" Maudsleigh Dudley and wife Philippa arrived in New York on 'SS Olympic'. Their home address was 78 Regents Park Road in Finchley London. As "Jack Dudley" he was still at that address in 1916. In 1914 Maudsleigh was writing from England as an Australian to denounce disparaging comments about Australia given by author Charles E. Jacomb.

In early October 1915 Estelle Dudley was featuring in English newspapers as a "little dancer of promise" who had been training from the age of 2½. Life was less rosy for her father. On October 28th 1915 the 'Globe' reported that Maudsleigh John Dudley had appeared in the Bankruptcy Court. He was described as a “professional backer of horses” who lived in Regent’s Park Road. Since the outbreak of war, racing in Britain had been curtailed and stopped in France and Belgium. His business supplying sandwiches to city workers had likewise failed. As director of a theatrical syndicate he had his production withdrawn within a fortnight after zeppelin raids and the Lusitania disaster. He had also sustained stock exchange losses, and had liabilities of £1,540 with no assets of value.

In December 1917 Estelle Dudley was creating a sensation as ‘Alice in Wonderland' at the ‘Savoy Theatre’ in London. Her proud father posted her birth certificate in the theatre foyer for those who could not credit such a youngster with the “histrionic ability” and “great cleverness and versatility” displayed. The production was still touring England in January 1919, and Estelle reportedly earned £100 per week. In 1919 Leslie Dudley won a certificate from the ‘London Royal Drawing Society’ for his designs of aeroplanes, submarines and zeppelins (in adulthood he became an engineer).

In February 1920 Estelle had composed a charming waltz that was published in London. In April 1920 she was conducting the orchestra at the ‘London Coliseum' while they performed her composition. In October 1920 the family arrived in New York on 'SS Aquitania’ on their way to Sydney. Maudsleigh John Dudley was an "author" and Estelle an "actress". Their home address was "3 Spanish Place Mansions Manchester Square London”.

On March 27th 1921 they arrived back in London from Sydney on 'Ormonde' after a tour of China, Japan and India.

On April 6th 1921 officers from Scotland Yard arrested Maudsley John Dudley "commission agent" (bookmaker) of Spanish Place Mansions in London. Two other men were also arrested, in connection with a conspiracy to obtain money by false pretenses perpetrated back in July 1920. Major Ballantyne Alexander Large had at that time parted with £2,300 in a scam horse racing betting scheme. Dudley was identified as an undischarged bankrupt but he lived sumptuously. He represented himself as a financier, dabbler in stocks and shares and a former racehorse owner. By early May other charges involving card games and an "infallible betting scheme" that defrauded David Kinnear Hall of some £25,000 were also brought against Dudley (and others). The three separate offences took place in 1919. At London's 'Old Bailey' on July 14th 1921 the confidence trickster was sentenced to five years in prison for obtaining large sums of money by betting and card tricks.

The 'UK Register of Habitual Criminals' lists Dudley's 1897, 1899, 1900 and 1902 convictions in Australia for larceny, false pretenses and conspiracy. He was also expelled from Johannesburg South Africa in 1905 for contravening permit laws. He was born in Australia, and known aliases were Joseph Palmer and Jack Dudley. He is described as 5'8¾" in height with grey eyes and a wart on his left cheek. He was liberated from 'Parkhurst Prison' on March 20th 1925.

While her father served his time in prison, Estelle Dudley made a name for herself on the vaudeville stage in America from at least October 1922. Given her age, her mother probably accompanied her. By September 1926 the “Queen of Jazz" had left her association with the "Four Dance Lords" although in November 1926 she was still in vaudeville in America as “Estelle Dudley & Co”. She appears to have retired from the stage soon after this.

In 1925 Mrs. Philippa Dudley’s home address was still registered as “3 Spanish Place Mansions” in London. Whether Maudsley ever returned to her is not known, but by February 1926 he was in Paris under the alias John Martin Davidson. By December 1926 Swiss authorities had issued a warrant for his arrest, and even Australian Police Gazettes were advertising for his apprehension. With two other criminals he was accused of stealing 180,000 Dutch guilders in 1,000 guilder notes (£18,000) from a Dutch merchant in August 1926, through a confidence trick involving the purchase of shares. A reward of 4,000 Swiss francs as well as 10% of the amount recovered was payable to the person who located him. One of the accused was prosecuted in London and awaited extradition to Switzerland, but his role in the affair was questioned and the case appears to have been dropped. Dudley was never apprehended.

In July 1927 Estelle Dudley traveled on 'Berengaria' from England to New York. She was still single, had no occupation and her home address was "6 Grays Inn Square" in London. In August 1928 (now as Estelle Magdalen Dudley) she traveled on 'Conte Biancamano' from Genoa Italy to New York. She still had no occupation and her last permanent address was in Cannes France. On October 21st 1928 she arrived in Glasgow from New York on ‘Caledonia’ with her father, who was calling himself Lionel John Dudley. He was described as a ‘financier’ while she had no occupation. Estelle intended to settle in England but he did not. In September 1940 Estelle Dudley spoke (in French) on radio in Los Angeles about her experiences. She had lived in Europe for fifteen years and served as the head of the ambulance corps with the regular French army during the war.

In 1927 Philippa Victoria Dudley (nee Ellis) married art dealer Gerald Walton Reynell in London. In that year Leslie Clarence Dudley was an electrical engineering student living in Edgbaston. In 1939 the Reynells lived in Queens Gate Kensington. Gerald was a miniature portrait specialist and Philippa was a housewife who often traveled. Leslie Clarence married in Kensington in 1934, and in 1939 he was living in Shrewsbury in Shropshire and working as an electrical and mechanical engineer for the 'Ministry of Supply'. He emigrated to America and 1957 and was naturalized in 1962, taking up the name “Leslie Peter Dudley”. At that time he lived in Wilshire Boulevard in Los Angeles and worked as a consultant optical engineer. Philippa Reynell died in Ealing London in April 1966, leaving assets of £1,591. Gerald Reynell died in Ealing in August 1966 leaving assets of £3,247. Leslie Peter Dudley died in Hounslow London in 1986. Estelle married Surrey native David William Pennick (Lieutenant of the Royal Navy) in Kensington in 1946 and died in Epsom Surrey in early 1951.

After his escape from justice for the fraud in Zurich in 1926, Dudley used the first names Lionel, Lionel John, Lionel John Gibson and Hamilton and traveled constantly. He represented himself as a financier or an author and had become considerably younger. He said he was born in Canada. As mentioned above, in October 1928 he traveled with his daughter Estelle from New York to Glasgow. In April 1928 he traveled from Palermo to New York on 'Saturnia'. He may have arrived in New York on July 13th 1928 from Naples on 'Conte Biancamano' (ship manifests show him arriving in Plymouth from Gibraltar on 'Narkunda' on the same day!). On July 22nd 1928 he arrived in Canada on 'Atholl' from Liverpool and was to stay at the 'Hotel Mount Royal' in Montreal.

Dudley's future "wife" Cecile Helen Grey, a wealthy widow who had been born in Venice Italy in 1892, made her first visit to Canada in June 1928. They appear to have embarked together at Southampton on May 18th 1929 and traveled on 'Aquitania' to New York. Their passports were issued in different places at different times and their home addresses were different. Cecile lived at 26 Cockspur Street London and Dudley at "The Hall" Bushey in Hertfordshire (both were probably hotels). It is likely that they had only recently met (or perhaps they met on board).

In March 1930 Lionel and Cecile Dudley traveled from Honolulu to Los Angeles on 'SS President Cleveland'. He was still a "financier". In September 1932 when they traveled on 'Maloja' from Marseilles to Tilbury they were living at the 'Hotel Belgravia' in London (this time he was an "author"). On December 21st 1932 Hamilton and Cecil Dudley embarked at London upon 'Viceroy of India' for a pleasure cruise. They now lived at the 'Metropole Hotel' in London. When they sailed on 'Mohawk' from Havana to Florida in January 1933 he was an "author". In late November 1933 they sailed from Bombay to Gibraltar on 'Rajputana' and home was still the 'Metropole Hotel'.

In September and October 1933 a distinguished Indian gentleman named Sir Albion Banerji, who now lived in England, was defrauded of £4,600 after meeting three confidence tricksters on a cross-channel steamer on August 4th 1933. The victim was supposedly buying shares in 'Union Consolidated Mining Company' of Nevada. By November 1st 1934 the author Maudsleigh John Dudley had been identified as one of the three fraudsters and was committed at Marlborough Police Court in London to stand trial. He reportedly posed as a lawyer in West End hotels in London.

At London's 'Old Bailey' on November 15th 1934 Dudley pleaded guilty to conspiring with others to defraud through false pretenses. The court was told that Dudley's share of the money was only £840 and that he had gone to America hoping to sell some of his literary work in Hollywood but had been arrested in New Orleans. He was sentenced to two years with hard labour and six months for making a false statement when procuring a passport, the sentences to be served concurrently. Newspapers of the day reported that

Dudley had previously written songs and stories whilst in 'Parkhurst Prison'.

Cecile Helen continued to travel using both first names and both surnames during Dudley's incarceration. On ship manifests her contacts were Mrs. Jessie Beatty (a foster sister) in New York and Mrs. Burchell in Baker Street London (a cousin). In 1936 she was living at 'Grosvenor House' in London. By April 8th 1937 Maudsleigh Dudley had been released from prison. On that day he and Cecil Dudley departed Liverpool on 'Reine del Pacifico' bound for Nassau in the Bahamas. He had reverted to his correct age and was an author living with Cecile at "Dudley House" in Southampton Street London.

For the 1939 UK census Dudley had become John Egerton (author) and he was living at "Nell Gwyn House" 547 Sloane Avenue Chelsea in London with Helen Grey (a gentlewoman of independent means). She was widowed and he was divorced. Their specific birth dates are listed – Helen as October 10th 1892 and his as November 12th 1875 (exactly the same as that of John Joseph Coghlan in Sydney).

On November 4th 1940 John Egerton (also registered under John Maudsleigh Dudley) of the above address died at the 'Kingthorpe Nursing Home' in Addlestone Surrey. Probate to his "widow" Helen was £16 16s 7d. Cecil Helen Grey (also registered under Dudley and Helen Egerton) died at the 'Windsor Hotel' in London on

January 31st 1944. Her assets were substantially greater at £1,937 19s 6d.

And what of the birth family of John Joseph Coghlan? His mother Josephine Theresa (nee Murphy) died in Sydney in 1908. A sister Nora E. Coghlan (born in 1886) married Ernest Keen in Sydney in 1913. A brother Leo Francis Coghlan (born June 6th 1881) emigrated to America in 1907 and settled in Portland Oregon, where he died in July 1948. In 1920 he had worked as a domestic servant in Manhattan. In 1930 he was a janitor in Portland. In 1940 he was a hotel window cleaner in Portland and was still unmarried. Unregistered births (with names unknown) born to John Francis and Josephine Coghlan in Sydney were a daughter on January 9th 1878, twin sons on February 9th 1880 and a daughter in September 1883.

Leslie Dudley 1912

John James Coghlan Sydney 1897

John James Coghlan alias Cranston Hobart 1899

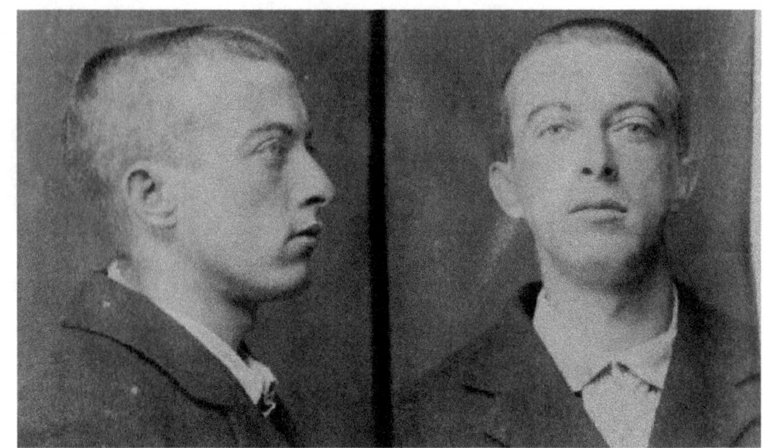

John Coghlan alias Palmer Melbourne 1900

Estelle Dudley 1915

Estelle & Philippa Dudley 1921

MAUDSLEY JOHN DUDLEY.

Maudsley John Dudley 1926

Reginald Stanley Charlton Collins(1885-1962)

Reginald was the eldest son of Thomas Jones Collins (accountant) and Emma Clara Charlton, born at Paddington in Sydney on December 12th 1885. A sister Vida Winifred was born in October 1883 and younger brother Herbert Leslie in January 1888.

When Thomas Jones Collins died suddenly of a brain hemorrhage at Paddington on July 17th 1908, obituaries may give some clue as to why Reginald later behaved as he did. Did Reginald feel overlooked by his father? The "genial, generous and enthusiastic" Thomas had been an art and photography enthusiast and was also keen on cricket and football. The 'Australian Star' of July 20th 1908 notes that Thomas was proud of the prowess of his son Herbert as first grade bowler for the 'Paddington District Cricket Club'. Herbert's cricket skills outshone Reginald's from an early age (Herbie played for and eleven times captained the 'Australian Test Cricket Team' from 1920 until 1926). In July 1908 Reg worked as a clerk with the 'Sydney City Council', Vida was married to Alexander McCarthy of the 'Commonwealth Crown Law Department', and Herbie worked for brewers 'Tooth & Co." A weakness that beset both Reginald and Herbert as adults (but not apparently their father) was an addiction to gambling. For Reginald this led to criminal activity, while Herbert was sustained by his cricket abilities and connections during tough times.

On June 1st 1911 Reginald Stanley Collins married Violet (Poppy) Westgarth. 'Truth' (Sydney) of May 23rd 1937 notes that Miss Poppy Westgarth was "one of the loveliest blondes Sydney has ever known" so it is a pity that I am unable to discover a photo of her at any age. A daughter Violet Roslyn Collins was born on June 27th 1912, with a proud announcement in the 'Sydney Morning Herald' recording the event at the couple's residence 'Girrahween' in Double Bay.

On August 23rd 1915 Reginald Stanley Collins (clerk at Sydney Town Hall) signed up for the war with the army. He and Violet were then living at 72 Newcastle Street Rose Bay. Military records show his height as 5'8¾" and his eye colour as grey. The 'Sydney Morning Herald' of July 7th 1916 noted that Reginald had left Sydney some months earlier as a warrant officer with the 'Army Service Corps', had been promoted to Lieutenant and was now in France. The 'Referee' (Sydney) of July 19th 1916 describes him as the brother of H.L. Collins NSW batsman.

Once Reginald left for overseas on November 18th 1915 it is most likely that Violet Collins and her daughter moved to 'Fig Tree House' on the Lane Cove River to be with her widowed mother Lucy Florence Westgarth (nee Mansfield). We know that when Lucy left there in 1918 and rented a flat in Manning Road Double Bay, Violet Collins and her daughter moved there too. Violet "Poppy" Westgarth had been brought up firstly in the mansion 'St. Helens' at Campbelltown built in 1887 by her solicitor father George Charles Westgarth. When he died of tuberculosis in October 1908, his widow Lucy Florence was forced to sell St. Helens to pay for debts and look after her five sons and four daughters. By the end of 1909 she had rented a large house on the Lane Cove River and established a school for girls (where Poppy was still able to keep company with the daughters of city elites and landed gentry).

Reginald Stanley Collins was finally demobbed from the 'Australian Army' in London in December 1920, and formally discharged with the rank of 'Captain' (as Staff Officer of A.I.F. Personnel) on April 26th 1921. Living in Knightsbridge London in 1921, he had decided not to return home, probably because Herbie was spending much of his time in England with cricket. In 1919 Herbert captained the 'A.I.F. XI' team touring England and from December 1920 he played with the 'Australian Test Cricket Team' (having been demobbed from the army in March 1920). Reginald wrote to his wife admitting to adultery with another woman in August 1919 at the 'Hyde Park Hotel' in London. He declared that he had lost all affection for Violet and had resigned his position at Sydney's Town Hall. In April 1921 Violet in Sydney sued for divorce from Reginald on the grounds of his adultery with an unknown woman.

By February 1926 Reginald Collins was working in the Civil Service in London in the 'Clearing Office, Enemy Debts', and captaining the 'Civil Service Cricket Team' whilst his brother captained the 'Australian Test Cricket Team'. On March 25th 1926 he was described as an "accountant" living at the 'Rembrandt Hotel' when he married Ellen Mary Adam at 'Holy Trinity Church' in

Brompton. From Eastbourne in Surrey, Ellen (known as "Lal") was twenty years younger than her husband.

Life was progressing swimmingly for Reginald Stanley Collins at this stage. In 1934 he took up duties with the 'Board of Trade' and in August and September 1936 he and Ellen traveled to Canada and America on 'Empress of Britain' and 'Queen Mary'. Their address was now 'Maryfield' 56 Princes Way Wimbledon Park in London, and Reginald was variously described as a civil servant or an accountant. In 1939 and 1940 they were still at that address, and in street directories Reginald had started denoting himself as "Captain". By 1942 they were living at St James's Court Buckingham Gate and things had taken a turn for the worse.

In March 1942 Reginald Stanley Collins failed, with liabilities of £14,934 and net assets of £4,827 and he was suspended from the Civil Service. He was examined by the 'London Bankruptcy Court' in May 1942, where he happily agreed that he was unable or unwilling to break free from keeping up sham appearances, and said that his extravagant ways went back to his army days when as an officer he made social connections with wealthy people. His salary had reached £860 per annum, but over the last three years his personal and household expenditure was £9,000. He spent over £1,000 per year on himself and his wife certainly spent more than that on her own personal expenses. She had been ill in 1940 and he had incurred medical expenses as a consequence. When his salary was £7,000 per annum he had bought a house and land at Wimbledon (56 Princes Way) for £5,000 and kept two maids. He borrowed from friends, bankers and moneylenders, speculated on the stock exchange and visited casinos on the Continent.

There were allegations in the 'Bankruptcy Court' on May 20th 1942 that Collins had obtained money from creditors through dealing in wines and spirits. He denied this and declared that he had merely borrowed the money. Nothing further came of this until June 1944. By this time he was living at the 'Royal Court Hotel' in Sloane Square Chelsea London, and probably had parted from Ellen Mary (in divorce proceedings on the grounds of her desertion in July 1948 it was stated that they last lived together at Buckingham Gate). At Bow Street Police Court, Reginald (now purportedly employed as an accountant by a firm of newsagents) was charged with obtaining sums of £850 and £320 from Arthur Edward Beach, £600 from Leopold Etrioni and £1,000 from Herbert Mackenzie in early 1941 through deals in wines and spirits. He was sentenced to six months imprisonment.

Happily for Ellen Mary Collins (nee Adam) she came from a good family (as had Reginald's first wife). Her widowed mother of 'Clifton Lodge' in Epsom Road Guildford died in April 1945, leaving an estate of £5,437 9s to be shared between Ellen (Lal) and her married sister Violet Estelle (Stella) Grimston. Both probably lived at 'Clifton Lodge' until around 1950. When Ellen arrived back on 'Rangitiki' from an overseas trip in December 1952, her address was that of Violet and her husband's now in Hove Sussex. When Ellen died on October 20th

1964 she lived at 280 Dyke Road Brighton in Sussex and her estate of £19,871 was left to Violet. When Violet died in 1983 she left an estate of £68,547 and her address was now 280 Dyke Road. Her husband (retired Lieutenant Colonel George Sylvester Grimston) died in 1990, also at this address, leaving a large estate of £147,580. In his youth he was reportedly a first class cricketer, so perhaps Reginald met Ellen through cricket connections.

Having followed the second wife of Reginald Stanley Collins to her death, it is timely to revisit his relatives back in Australia. Vida Winifred McCarthy (nee Collins) died in Sydney in December 1924, as the "dearly loved" daughter of Emma Collins of 'Coleraine' in O'Brien Street Bondi and "loving sister" of Herbert L. Collins (no mention of Reginald). While Ellen Collins never remarried, Violet (Poppy) Collins married Gerald Wilfred Kemmis in Sydney in April 1927. In October 1933 the couple opened an up-market boarding house called 'Greentrees' in Bowral, and 'Truth' (Sydney) on February 3rd 1935 reported upon the engagement of Violet Roslyn Collins/Kemmis to Polish photographer Rene Pardon. Roslyn was apparently "just as pretty as her youthful looking mamma". Violet (Poppy) Kemmis and her daughter Violet Roslyn Pardon both led successful lives, dying in Sydney respectively in 1980 and 1985.

Herbie Collins (dubbed "Horseshoe" in luckier early days) retired from cricket in 1927. In August 1926 as captain of the 'Australian Test Cricket Team' playing in

England, there were suggestions that he had "thrown" the match by using an inexperienced bowler. Despite his reputation as a rabid gambler, there was however never any material evidence that Herbie ever fixed a cricket match. Suffering from neuritis and arthritis, Herbie made his debut as a bookmaker at Ascot in England in mid-October 1927. He then immediately returned to Sydney to set up permanently as a bookmaker and to look after his widowed mother Emma. He frequented all night poker sessions at Kings Cross, and eventually won and lost two fortunes on the racetrack. Around 1932 he was so poor that he sometimes went without food and required assistance from the 'NSW Cricketers Fund' to support him and his invalid mother. On October 2nd 1939 Emma died in Darlinghurst, and Herbert was gracious enough to include his brother in the newspaper tribute to her as the "dearly loved mother of R.S. and H.L. Collins" although it is doubtful that Reginald ever assisted the family financially. Failing as a bookmaker, Herbert Leslie Collins finally became a commission agent for punters and bookies. He died of lung cancer in Sydney in May 1959.

Returning to Reginald Stanley Collins, who had been sentenced to six months in prison in London in 1944, we find him upon his release living in 'Devere Gardens' Kensington then for several years at 'Baileys Hotel' in Kensington before moving to 'Nell Gwynn House' in Chelsea by the time of his divorce in July 1948. When he stood in court at London's 'Old Bailey' in December 1950 he described himself as an accountant living at 'Harrington Gardens' in South Kensington.

In fact, he had been living in luxury since his release from prison by extracting money from women into whose affections he had worked his way. His five victims, who all lived in the Chelsea area, were told that he owned vast estates in Australia and a £7,000 house in Wimbledon, and was to receive £38,000 in a divorce settlement. The women were persuaded to advance money for investments in shares and business deals. Miss Williams, who lost £8,000 to the scoundrel with "a flair for writing love letters", said that "Captain Collins of the Treasury" (as he now styled himself) spent most of his money at greyhound tracks but was "the worst backer in the world". She found him, however, "a most charming companion" who was able to converse easily on music, painting and drama (possibly thanks to his father's interest in these areas).

Following an initial complaint from one of his victims, Reginald had disappeared, but subsequently paid a small bill at a West End restaurant with a dud cheque. He was thus traced to a West End hotel, and was found by police in bed at midday. He had an outstanding bill for £19 19s 4d but only 2d in his pocket. All his expensive clothes had been pawned. He was described as a "neat, bald-headed little man in gold rimmed glasses, who always carried an immaculate umbrella". Collins pleaded guilty to thirty-seven offences against the women. The ten charges involved obtaining money by false pretenses, fraudulent conversions and obtaining credit while an undischarged bankrupt. In total he had received over £12,000 through these scams. On December 18th 1950 he was sentenced to four years imprisonment.

The last mention that I can find of Reginald is in the 'Sunday Mirror' (UK) on April 15th 1956. Now calling himself Reginald Charlton Collins, he was gambling at the casino in Monte Carlo. The sarcastic article notes that he tells people he is an official of Her Majesty's Treasury currently on sick leave, that he played cricket for Middlesex and last week taught Winston Churchill to play baccarat. His death in Islington, London in early 1962 was recorded under the names Reginald S. C. Collins and Reginald S. Charlton-Collins. There is no sign of any estate to probate.

Mail (Adelaide, SA : 1912 - 1954), Saturday 10 July 1926, page 32

AUSTRALIAN CAPTAIN'S BROTHER WEDS. — Captain Reginald S. Collins, brother of H. L. Collins, the captain of the Australian Test Team, was married in London recently

AUSTRALIA'S CRICKET CAPTAIN'S BROTHER MARRIED
MR. R. COLLINS (CENTRE) AND MISS H. M. ADAMS

English Newspaper Version 1926

Herbie "Horseshoe" or "Lucky" Collins

▲ St Helen's Park House, on the Appin Road at Campbelltown, is a high Victorian mansion with the Gothic influence of the period showing in the elaborate arrangement of gables with their intricate fretwork bargeboards. It was built in 1887 of local Menangle sandstone.

Above: Early childhood home of Violet Westgarth
Below: Fig Tree House School home of Violet Westgarth before her marriage to Reginald Collins

Arthur Coningham (1863-1939)

Arthur was born on July 14th 1863 at Emerald Hill in Melbourne, the youngest child in the family and the only one born in Australia. In August 1861 the rest of the family, consisting of Jane Ann (nee Wilson), eldest son William James, daughter Jane Elizabeth and son Walter had arrived in Melbourne on 'Clutha'. Earlier in the year these four were living at Limehouse in London, where although William John Coningham is absent Jane is listed as a "brass founder's wife".

William John Coningham (Arthur's father) married Jane Ann Wilson on April 1st 1855 in London (he was a "brass finisher"). In 1851 William was still at home with his birth family in Colt Street Limehouse, and was an "optician's apprentice". His older brothers were already successfully employing workers under them, while his father George William Coningham was always listed in census records as a "Parish Beadle" for Limehouse. Presumably he received some payment for the prominent church position, but prior to January 1851 George also ran a printing business (in partnership) and on the 1855 marriage record for his son William he is shown as a "baker". George was prosperous to enough to employ domestic servants in his later years. He died at Limehouse in December 1890.

Jane Ann Wilson (Arthur's mother) came from an even more prosperous family. In 1851 she was still living at home at 'Brighton House' in Bromley St Leonard in London, and her father James was a brickmaker who employed thirty-four men. He died at 'Danbury House' in Essex on May 25th 1871 and apparently left a large estate (chiefly freehold property) that was to be divided between twenty-four beneficiaries. Probate to administer the estate was granted to his wife Mary Elizabeth, but she had done little or nothing before her death in Loughton Essex on May 4th 1874. Confusion now reigned, with Mary's estate to be administered by her son James William Wilson (brickmaker) while the administration of her late husband's estate was given to tobacconist Benjamin Thomas Wilson (the son of one of the residuary legatees).

In late 1927 the Chancery Division of the High Court in England was trying to locate the remaining three unpaid beneficiaries of the estate of James Wilson, namely Arthur Coningham, his brother Walter (deceased by then) and his sister Jane Elizabeth (Jenny) Dugdale (nee Coningham) who was believed to have left Australia for England many years earlier (I cannot trace her after May 1898 when she was sailing on 'Lake Huron' with her husband William Dugdale from England to Montreal Canada). As early as November 1884 authorities had been attempting to find Jane Ann Coningham (nee Wilson) in Australia.

By December 1882 the cricket prowess of young Arthur Coningham was being mentioned in Melbourne newspapers. At that time he played for the 'Brighton Terminus' Team. In December 1884 he moved to Queensland and represented that state at cricket from February 1885. From December 1892 he also played for

New South Wales, and from February 1896 until December 1898 he played for New South Wales and for the 'Australian Eleven' in international matches. The 'Clarence River Advocate' of January 4th 1901 describes Arthur's career as an all-round sportsman. In 1882 in Melbourne he won several pigeon shooting matches. In 1883-1884 he won the 'Melbourne Cricket Club' bowling trophy and gained a medal for saving a life in Hobson's Bay. When he played cricket for the 'Australian Eleven' in England in 1893 he managed to receive yet another medal for saving a boy's life in the Thames River. Renowned as "eccentric" and a "joker", during a match at Blackpool Arthur was cold while fielding and started a fire on the outfield using straw and twigs to keep himself warm. Between 1885 and 1889 he was winning hurdle and running races in Brisbane. He also dabbled in football and was a "smart billiard player".

Arthur moved states for his cricket. In 1895 he was listed in the Brisbane City Directory as a "chemist" living at Cordelia Street South Brisbane. Later that year he moved back to Sydney. All three sons of William John Coningham qualified to practice as chemists. William James Coningham was working as a chemist in Chiltern Victoria by 1883. Walter Coningham qualified in 1889 and moved to Queensland (where he married in that year) to practice. In 1890 Arthur was working as a chemist for 'Prosser, Taylor & Co' in Brisbane.

It is probable that William John and Jane Ann Coningham settled in Sydney by 1888, along with son William James and daughter Jane Elizabeth. William

James (chemist) died at Marrickville on December 11th 1893. Jane Elizabeth married William Dugdale in Sydney in 1894. Walter remained in Queensland, working as a chemist at Pentland for some years before moving to Charters Towers around 1899. He died there in October 1902, leaving a wife and five children. Jane Ann Coningham (nee Wilson) died at her residence 89 Watkins Street Newtown in Sydney on August 4th 1898 (at which time Arthur was living in Glebe Road Glebe). After his wife's death William John Coningham moved to Queensland, and from 1903 he worked as a plumber and gasfitter in Townsville until he died there (intestate) in September 1912.

Until scandal erupted in late 1900, Arthur Coningham was the shining star in his family. Then living in Sydney, he was unable to practice as a pharmacist because he was not registered in New South Wales. He was a registered chemist and druggist in Queensland, and the 'Clarence River Advocate' of January 4th 1901 noted that once the 'Federal Reciprocal Treaty' was agreed between the Pharmacy Boards of the various colonies it was expected that Arthur would be able to practice in Sydney. Given his financial woes in Sydney, it is inexplicable to me that he did not return to Brisbane to practice as a qualified chemist (more of this later).

Arthur Coningham's choice of wife is just as inexplicable as his decision to remain in Sydney. English-born Alice Stamford Dowling moved to Brisbane as a teenager, in 1886. Her father, a warrant officer with the British Army, died at Petrie Terrace in Brisbane in November 1890.

Here mother Rachael and married sister Mary Bostock were still with her in Brisbane, and it was around this time that she met Arthur Coningham. In April 1887 Alice gave birth to an illegitimate child registered as Cecil Charles Dowling, but the boy died in November of that year. To disguise her unmarried status, Alice went by the name of Mrs. Rogers, and Arthur later testified that he did not know about the child or why she called herself Mrs. Rogers (she said it was for business reasons).

Even before their marriage, there were issues over their opposing church allegiances. They were in Sydney in March 1893 when a Catholic priest agreed to marry them in the parlour of his presbytery in Paddington. Not allowed to marry in a Catholic Church because Arthur was a Protestant, Alice obtained a dispensation to marry him and he agreed that their children would be brought up as Catholics. Arthur was about to leave for England with the 'Australian Eleven' cricket team and at the last moment he refused to go through with the ceremony. He offered to give her money while he was away and promised to marry her on his return. Alice would not let it go, and on March 11th 1893 they married in 'St. Matthew's Anglican Church' at Bondi. He left for England the same day, to return seven months later, and Alice returned to live with her mother in Brisbane.

The birth of Arthur Coningham Junior at Cordelia Street in Brisbane on January 19th 1895 was proudly proclaimed in newspapers. In December 1895 reports stated that Arthur would move to Sydney because the 'New South Wales Cricket Association' would pay his expenses for intercolonial matches, while the 'Queensland Cricket Association' would not. In January 1896 he was given a permit to play for the 'South Sydney Club', and opened a tobacconist, hairdressing and sports depot shop in Waverley. Daughter Mabel Frances was born on May 9th 1896 but Arthur was declared insolvent as of September 14th 1896 (he complained he received insufficient patronage from the Waverley locals, and that he was owed money earned through playing billiards in Brisbane and from the 'Queensland Cricket Association'). Arthur now moved to join the 'Glebe Cricket Team' and began managing a tobacconist shop at 131 Glebe Road Glebe. In December he was allowed to leave the colony to play with the 'New South Wales Cricket Team'. He was living in Wigram Road Glebe Point, and fainted in Bankruptcy Court under considerable signs of nervous strain. He earned money as a professional cricketer to repay his creditors, and in July 1897 he was discharged from bankruptcy.

In December 1898 Arthur Coningham was still working at the tobacconist and hairdressers shop at 131 Glebe Road Glebe when it was destroyed by fire (it was insured). By February 1899 he had left the 'Glebe Cricket Team' and taken a shop at 141 King Street East Sydney, whilst living in Woollahra. Owing to residential requirements he did not play much club cricket now. He obtained a registered license for the sale of tobacco, cigars and cigarettes but seems to have been restless. In October 1899 newspapers noted that after trying many occupations "Connie" had taken to bookmaking at Randwick Racecourse in Sydney. With his "system" he wore a bag around his neck labeled “Coningham the Cricketer”. On January 22nd 1900 he left for Brisbane to work as a special representative of the ‘Equitable Life Assurance Company of USA’. In March 1900 Arthur was playing well for the ‘Nundah Cricket Team’. He returned to Sydney on May 14th 1900, to the house in Fairfield where his family was living with Alice’s mother and sister Mary Bostock, and soon was to say that he found his wife acting strangely.

On September 27th 1900 Arthur Coningham (now described as a chemist of Darlinghurst) petitioned for divorce from Alice and named Catholic priest Rev. Dr. Denis Francis O’Haran as co-respondent. He was seeking £5,000 in damages from O’Haran for the maintenance and education of his children Arthur and Mabel Frances (asking for custody) and this necessitated a trial by special jury. On October 17th 1900 Dr. O'Haran filed his answer to the suit, denying the allegations. The adultery was said to have occurred in buildings adjacent to St. Mary’s Cathedral between June 15th 1898 and September 30th 1899 and Alice had reportedly admitted to such. Arthur looked through Alice’s possessions on May 23rd 1900 after his return from Brisbane and found an autographed photo of O’Haran and two green harps such as are sold in the streets on St. Patrick’s Day. He taxed her with misconduct and she then allegedly told him the whole story.

John Henry Want Q.C. representing Dr. O’Haran stated that after his wife's "confession" Arthur did not immediately file for divorce. Instead, he wrote three times to Cardinal Moran issuing threats about publicizing the adultery using posters and was keen to settle for damages out of court. Receiving no reply, he tried Dr. O'Haran himself. Want suggested that Arthur Coningham had a need for money and coerced his wife in a conspiracy to extort thousands from O'Haran or his employer. Until Arthur filed for divorce, he and Alice still lived together. The real victim in the case was young Vincent Francis Coningham, born on November 11th 1899 and now alleged to be O'Haran's child. Vincent was baptized at St. Mary's Cathedral on December 28th 1899 and the birth was registered on January 6th 1900. Here the father was listed as Arthur Coningham of 46 Grafton Street Woollahra. Much was made in court of Vincent's second name as being "homage" to O'Haran (Alice said he was named after the doctor who delivered him) and of Alice's indiscretions before her marriage.

The divorce trial became a battle between Catholic and Protestant ideologies and Alice asserted that the adultery took place on Friday nights so that O'Haran could cleanse himself of his sin at confession on Saturdays. Arthur's initial solicitor in the case, Ernest Abigail, was arrested on a charge of attempting to persuade Thomas Coogan to give false evidence, and could not continue with the case whilst under committal (he was subsequently acquitted by a jury without being called upon for his defense). Arthur next employed Hiram Asa Moss to represent him, but when Mr. Want obtained a confession from Arthur that he had continued to share a room with Alice after the divorce petition was filed (at Mrs. Bray's boarding house in Park Road Moore Park and at Mrs. Abraham's boarding house at 46 Alberto Terrace Darlinghurst) Moss withdrew from the case and Arthur represented himself. Arthur asserted that he shared rooms with Alice to save money but they kept separate beds.

Alice confessed on oath in court to her adultery with Dr. O'Haran. She had told her husband of her pregnancy with Vincent on June 13th 1899. Arthur declared that he could not have fathered the child in February 1899 because he was suffering from an injury by a cricket ball (although they were sleeping together). Why then did he register himself as Vincent's father on January 6th 1900? The first trial concluded on December 14th 1900, with the all-Protestant jury unable to agree. Eight members of the jury believed O'Haran and four believed the Coninghams.

The second trial began on Monday March 11th 1901, and Catholic forces had been busy gathering evidence from informers during the interim. Since October 1900 Arthur had been living with his old friend James Exton in Glenmore Road Paddington, while Alice and the children had moved from pillar to post and for a week in late February were at 'Burilda' boarding house in Fairfield (she under the name Mrs. Arnold). Arthur visited Alice there and sent her money, and once Alice was supposedly drunk enough to be carried up to bed.

Arthur Coningham and James Exton fell out and Arthur left Exton's house on March 11th 1901. Exton now provided testimony for O'Haran's defense team. Mr. Want produced letters and telegrams indicating conspiracy about testimony between Arthur (using James Exton's name without his knowledge according to Exton) and Alice (as Mrs. Arnold) but Arthur insisted that these were forgeries. On March 19th 1901, having left Exton's home, Arthur accused Exton of stealing a necklet valued at £2 from him on January 16th 1901. That case was dismissed on April 12th 1901 when Exton proved that he had paid eighty shillings for the necklet in late December 1900.

Both Arthur and Alice appeared to be confident and unembarrassed by their allegations in court. The divorce case concluded on April 2nd 1901, when the jury (two Roman Catholics, two Jews and eight Protestants) unanimously found that Dr. O'Haran had not committed adultery. They also found that there was insufficient evidence to prove conspiracy by the Coninghams. (According to some this indicated distaste for the means employed by O'Haran's defense team.) The judge agreed with the verdict and dismissed the co-respondent, whereupon Arthur sobbed and moaned, buried his face and then rushed at O'Haran. He ingloriously fell and was grabbed by the crowd.

The 'Australian Dictionary of Biography' describes Denis Francis O'Haran as paradoxically "both vain and self-effacing". At times he was "self-pitying and believing in his own importance" but he was "extremely charitable" and "very popular among parishioners". Cardinal Moran unequivocally believed in his innocence in the Coningham case. Funds were raised to cover O'Haran's substantial legal expenses. A religiously unbiased jury found him innocent of adultery, and I believe there is certainly evidence of collusion between Arthur and Alice in an attempt to blackmail or extort money. Why did she willingly give detailed evidence in court in the expectation that she would lose custody of Arthur and Mabel Frances, and blacken her own name and that of Vincent? Why hadn't Arthur taken the family back to Brisbane where he could earn money as a registered chemist, instead of living in poverty in Sydney?

In January 1901, prior to the second trial, Alice Coningham (perhaps anticipating excommunication) announced that she was leaving the Catholic Church and proposed to join the Church of England. On May 1st 1901, after the second trial, Arthur addressed a crowd of around two thousand in the 'Protestant Hall' in Sydney where a motion of sympathy with him was carried over his divorce case (but little money was raised). He announced that he was proceeding to New Zealand where he had obtained employment. His brother Walter was still in Queensland, and possibly his father William had also moved up there by now. Neither was involved with the divorce trials and perhaps Arthur was no longer in favour with them.

The 'Molong Argus' of May 3rd 1901 reported that the Coninghams were both living at Manly in Sydney (but apart). On May 4th 1901 Arthur departed on 'Warrimoo' for Wellington, leaving his family behind. In mid-May 1901 the 'Gisborne Times' announced that the recently arrived Mr. Coningham was likely to play for a local cricket club. In June he was touring the Wairarapa region as an agent for a life insurance company and buying and selling cash registers for the 'National Cash Register Company'. The 'Feilding Star' of June 14th noted that Arthur intended to re-open his divorce case when funds permitted.

In August 1901 Arthur returned to Sydney after traveling for an Insurance Society in New Zealand for three months. He was reportedly back in Wellington by October 1901. Sydney newspapers reported in May 1901 that Alice Coningham was working as a barmaid in a Sydney hotel. This was refuted in June (she was "living privately" i.e. supported by her husband) but resurrected in September, October and November. 'Punch' (Melbourne) on August 28th 1902 declared that Alice was still living in Manly and had tried to sell the story of her life but no publishers would take it. She then tried to hire a hall to deliver lectures on her controversial court cases, but was unsuccessful. At the same time Arthur was apparently back in Sydney attending religious revival services at the Town Hall.

In January 1903 there were reports that Arthur was intending to stand for parliament in New South Wales, but he was back in New Zealand by October and engaged as a coach by the 'North Shore Cricket Team'. In March 1903 Alice finally succeeded in delivering a series of lectures entitled 'Semper Eadem' at the 'Protestant Hall' in Sydney. Under the auspices of the 'Protestant Defence Association', the lectures were a general attack upon the Roman Catholic Church and the "tall, straight and slim to thinness" Alice proved to be "an elocutionist of some ability".

On November 11th 1903 Arthur Coningham was sentenced to six months in 'Hokitika Gaol' on charges of theft and false pretenses at Westport in New Zealand. He appealed to be allowed out on probation for the sake of his wife and three children, under the 'First Offenders Act'. The theft of three guineas was from his employer Robert Jason Innes (New Zealand representative for Sydney firm William Brooks & Company) on August 17th 1903. He was a traveling salesman selling 'Dr. Muscott's Medical Guide', working for wages and commissions and had sent the firm seven bogus orders to get his commissions (false pretenses) as well as converted payments received to his own use (theft). Coningham insisted that the case was merely a dispute over accounts. Evidence showed that Innes had told Coningham in Sydney that he would give him work if he came to New Zealand.

'Truth' (Sydney) on November 22nd 1903 noted that Innes testified to a verbal agreement to remit £2 per week to Coningham's wife in Sydney, which Innes did while Arthur continued to send in orders. He produced vouchers signed by Alice as receipts, while Arthur said he knew nothing of sending money and could not confirm her signature. Coningham was indebted to the firm for £105. Innes declared he and his company had received "shameful, lousy treatment" from the accused.

The 'New South Wales Police Gazette' of July 20th 1904 stated that a warrant had been issued by the 'Burwood Bench' in Sydney for the arrest of Arthur Coningham. Charged with wife desertion, he was described as 5'8" in height, of stout build with fair hair and moustache, blue eyes, a chemist or traveler and well-known cricketer. Alice's sister Mary Bostock and mother Rachael Dowling were now living in Burwood, and presumably Alice had returned to stay with them (Rachael died at Burwood in June 1911). In 1905 Arthur was back in the news in New Zealand, playing for the 'Newtown Cricket Club' and in "tip-top form". He lived in Wellington and worked as a commission agent. In 1908 he sued a woman for £136 over payment for his services as an agent in a mining business, and the judge concluded that his claim was ridiculous, extravagant and preposterous.

Vincent Orange (in his 1990 biography of Arthur Coningham Junior) states that by 1906 Alice and the children had moved to Wellington. In 1909 and 1910 young Arthur held free places at 'Wellington College', and was winning shooting championships but was often absent from school. He left college by November 1911 with no academic or technical qualifications. Mabel Frances continued her violin studies through 'Trinity College'.

In 1910 Alice was living in Fitzherbert Terrace Wellington while her husband was in Raumai working for 'W.T. Simons & Company'. In 1911 Alice was in rooms in an apartment block in Ghuznee Street Wellington while her husband was a "land agent" living at 319 The Terrace in Wellington. Alice (as Mrs. Stamford) was struggling to keep open a small ladies hairdressing business in Cuba Street with a man named Bennett. She and Arthur patched up their differences sufficiently to spend Christmas 1911 together, but early in the New Year Alice suspected that Arthur was having an affair with Mrs. Mary Ryman who lived in the same apartment block in Ghuznee Street. She hired a private detective, who found them together in a bathing shed on a beach at 'Lyall Bay' on January 19th 1912. It was Alice's turn to petition for divorce from Arthur.

This divorce hearing concluded on May 14th 1912. The jury unanimously found adultery on certain prescribed dates was proved, and the judge granted Alice a decree nisi with costs to Arthur and custody of the children to Alice. Counsel read out in court a letter from young Arthur to his father, complaining of his treatment of his mother and advising him to leave Wellington. He wrote, "Although you are my father, I am ashamed of you." Arthur senior intended to cross-petition Alice over alleged adultery with a dentist named Andrews, but this was dismissed in November 1912 after he failed to proceed with the petition.

With Arthur Senior out of their lives, Alice and the children prospered. Alice succeeded in her hairdressing business in Wellington, which became 'Stamford & Co' and Mabel joined the business to eventually become "company director". In October 1930 Mabel returned to Wellington after a grand tour of England, Europe and America, and Alice was shortly to leave for her own tour abroad. In that same year Vincent Francis qualified as a barrister in Wellington and set up his own business as a solicitor. The hairdressing business was sold in December 1936, and by the time of the 1939 UK Census Alice, Vincent and Mabel were all living together in Croydon Surrey. Alice was "incapacitated", Mabel was a lady's hairdresser with her own business and Vincent was a "solicitor and journalist". Alice died in Somerset England in 1959, Mabel (who never married) died in Somerset in 1980, and Vincent Francis (who never married) died in January 1983 in Somerset leaving a substantial estate of £64,791. All three lie together in a cemetery at Bicknoller in Somerset.

Arthur Coningham Junior joined New Zealand armed forces from August 1914 and served in Gallipoli and Egypt before becoming a flying ace with the English 'Royal Flying Corps' from 1916. His early nickname of "Maori" due to service in the New Zealand military later became "Mary". In 1932 he married the widow of a baronet. He himself was knighted on November 4th 1942 for his role in the Allied victory at El Alamein. In 1946 he was promoted to Air Marshal and appointed KBE, and he retired in 1947. He disappeared along with the other passengers and crew of 'Star Tiger' (British South American Airways) when it vanished without a trace on January 30th 1948 between the Azores and Bermuda (over the mysterious Bermuda Triangle). His estate was worth £5,451. He was a non-smoker, near teetotal and impatient with obscene language throughout his life.

We return to follow the life of Arthur Coningham Senior after his 1912 divorce. In 1914 he was living at 'King's Court' in East Auckland and working as a commercial traveler. On May 1st 1916 he enlisted for "Home Service" with the 'New Zealand Expeditionary Forces', at which time he was still living at 'King's Court' but stated he was a self-employed chemist. He listed all three children (including Vincent) as his own on the enlistment papers, and his contacts were Miss Goldman (a friend) in Sydney and his daughter at 'Stamford & Co' in Cuba Street in Wellington. He transferred to Rotorua in late July 1917. Historian Vincent Orange states that Arthur spent at least part of the war as a corporal in the 'Salvation Army' working at the 'Soldiers' Institute' there.

The last mention of Arthur in New Zealand is the 1919 electoral roll, where he is shown as a chemist living at Awahou in the Pohangina Valley. He had probably moved back to Sydney by 1925, when a newspaper reported that he "was not vastly impressed" with the quality of cricket at the Final Test between England and Australia at the 'Sydney Cricket Ground' in late February. In the 1930 electoral roll he is listed as a chemist living in Flinders Street Darlinghurst. In 1935 he was in Stephen Street North Randwick and had no occupation. On July 11th 1935 the 'Cumberland Argus and Fruitgrowers Advocate' reported that Arthur Coningham was living in the district and might play for the 'Central Cumberland Cricket Team' next year. In November 1937 Arthur was admitted to the 'Gladesville Mental Hospital' (the condition has not been disclosed to my knowledge) and he died there on June 13th 1939. His estate (in England and probably from the old James Wilson inheritance) was valued at £66 1s 9d and was left to his "widow" Alice Stamford Coningham.

Following his death, newspapers paid tribute to Arthur's outstanding cricket abilities in his glory days, and largely ignored the subsequent scandals. Arthur Coningham lies in 'Rookwood General Cemetery'.

Athur Coningham c. 1901

PRICE
SIXPENCE
"THE SENSATIONAL
CONINGHAM-O'HARAN TRIAL."
A full account of the most celebrated Divorce Case of the Nineteenth Century.
MRS CONINGHAM.
DR. O'HARAN.
ILLUSTRATED.

Sir Arthur "Mary" Coningham

Paul Darcy Fagan (1872-1919) and Gilbert Allan Fagan (1877-1942)

After the marriage of their mother Margaret Fagan (nee Dickens) to Henry/Harry Middleton in July 1885 in Melbourne Victoria, these brothers took on the surname of Middleton. Their sister Edith Annie Murray Fagan married dentist William St. John Stevens Davidson under the Fagan surname in Victoria in 1897.

In Melbourne in April 1871 Maggie Dickens (her father William was a plasterer) married reporter John Murray Fagan (born around 1848 to Thomas Fagan and Anne Murray who married in Victoria in 1841). Paul Darcy Gascoine Fagan (the firstborn) was born on January 28th 1872 in Fitzroy Melbourne. Other children died in infancy, with only Edith Annie (born in 1875) and Gilbert Allan Bertram (born in 1877) surviving to adulthood.

In 1871 John Murray Fagan was a newspaper publisher in Melbourne (this was probably the 'Melbourne Daily Telegraph'). In 1875, 1876 and 1877 he was a reporter/journalist. In 1878 he was a printer/compositor. He left Victoria in April 1879, and by December 1880 had supposedly left Temora in New South Wales for Narrandera or Bourke when he went missing. In March 1882 he was still missing, described as 5'10" in height with brown hair turning grey.

With three young children to take care of, Maggie Fagan became licensee of the 'Builders Arms Hotel' in Fitzroy by June 1883. She married Henry/Harry Middleton (born in Dunolly Victoria in 1858 and ten years younger than Maggie) by special license on July 28th 1885. Presumably this license was required because the whereabouts of John Fagan was still unknown. After the marriage Middleton became the licensee until August 1887. A son William Gibb Middleton was born but died in 1886. The couple then took over the 'Clifton Hotel' in Collingwood. On July 17th 1888 Maggie was admitted to the asylum at Kew suffering from mania. This sober and industrious woman had apparently been shocked when her supposedly dead husband Fagan walked into the bar about four months earlier, and had become suicidal, dangerous and destructive. Maggie Middleton (nee Dickens) was discharged from 'Kew Asylum' on June 3rd 1889 and died at Warburton in Victoria on November 29th 1892. She was buried at the St Kilda Cemetery. Henry's remarried mother Sarah Tucker who died in 1891 lies in the same grave as Maggie. After Maggie's death Henry Middleton can no longer be definitely traced. He does not lie in the same cemetery as his mother, wife or baby son. If it was John Murray Fagan who walked into the bar in 1888, I cannot discern what happened to him thereafter.

By the time of Maggie Middleton's death the grandparents of her children on all sides of the family had passed away. Gilbert was only fifteen years of age, Darcy twenty. We know that in late 1893 Gilbert Allan Middleton and a "Frederick J. Smith" (perhaps his brother Darcy?) were employed at the 'Standard Advertising Company' in Adelaide and boarding at

Glenelg. By January 17th 1894 they had left without paying their board but a criminal case against them was dismissed. In April 1894 Gilbert published a 'Bar Parlour Yarn' in a South Australian newspaper.

In June 1899 Gilbert Allan Middleton was partnered with a man named "Brooks" as advertising agents in Sydney New South Wales, when he sued a shopkeeper. In 1898 Darcy Middleton is listed in a Melbourne directory living in South Yarra, seemingly alone. By March 1901 Darcy Middleton is living in London under his own name with a Brisbane-born "wife" named "Louie" (no marriage record has been found) and others that included Gilbert under the alias of John Castles. They are described as "living off their own means". When they were arrested in April 1902 they were said to be well-known as "card sharpers" and "confidence men" in Melbourne, Adelaide and Sydney, but I can find no convictions in Australia. They reportedly left Australia around 1900 whilst on bail after a raid in Sydney related to horse racing or card sharping, and they were now running a luxuriously furnished suite of rooms near Buckingham Gate as a gaming house. Prior to April 1902 their depredations were said to have extended over two years as far as Eastbourne, Brighton and Cambridge.

At the Westminster Police Court on April 22nd 1902 it was asserted that none of the accused had ever before been charged with a criminal offence. At least one of the Middletons had traveled constantly on steamers between Melbourne and Sydney. On April 30th 1902 the gang members decided to plead guilty to keeping a gaming house. They were each sentenced to nine months in prison with hard labour.

After his release from prison Darcy Middleton assumed the name John Darlington Marsh. He reportedly met the elderly and extremely wealthy divorcee (and famous voice teacher) Sarah Hershey Eddy, who traveled much but was based in France, on a trans-Atlantic steamer where he was card-sharping. They married in Rye, Sussex on June 26th 1908 and Darcy had no more need of petty swindles after this. The marriage was "wholly unexpected by anyone" in Sarah's hometown of Muscatine in America. Sarah died suddenly of pneumonia in Paris in July 1911, at the age of seventy-four. The "Marshes" had been living at one of the finest country homes in France since their wedding. Sarah was survived by her husband (described as "an English gentleman of leisure and culture") a sister and a married daughter.

John Darlington Marsh wasted no time after his wife's death in leaving France. In October 1911 he traveled on 'Mauretania' to New York. In October 1913 he traveled with brother Gilbert (now also Marsh) from London to New York on 'Kaiserin Augusta Victoria'. On June 14th 1915 at Lewisburg West Virginia he married the widow of a banker and Texas "oil king" Ivor Tate O'Connor, born in 1876. Mr. Marsh of London and New York was "wealthy and not in business".

On December 4th 1916 the "pretty, stylishly-dressed" Ivor won a divorce from John Darlington Marsh, who since the marriage had traveled the globe with various female acquaintances. He did not contest the divorce suit and she did not request alimony. The papers were served on him in New York and he returned to London.

The 'Chicago Tribune' of September 10th 1917 described John Darlington Marsh as a "plunger, gambler and beneficiary of millions from his matrimonial and romantic exploits". He had once been a "dashing young person with much nerve and no money". He was an Australian who had originally played cards on trans-Atlantic steamers, and allegedly met Mrs. Eddy on such a steamer. After Sarah Hershey Eddy's death he had reportedly traded his villa in Nice for farmland in Iowa, and maintained contacts with his criminal mates in England.

John Darlington Marsh of 33 Savile Row London died on March 21st 1919 of pneumonia. Despite his earlier vast wealth, his estate (to be administered by Gilbert Marsh a racehorse owner living at Epsom) was only £244 10s 4d. He was buried in a grave at 'Epsom Cemetery' only a few yards from that of the actress Billie Carleton, who had died of a cocaine overdose in London in 1918. At the inquest into her death Marsh stated that he had known Billie for around six years and had given her large sums of money and most of her jewels. The five mourners at the graveside of Darcy Fagan/Middleton/Marsh included Gilbert (who had arranged both gravesites at Epsom) and his wife, although there were thirty wreaths and other floral tributes.

Turning now to Gilbert Allan Fagan/Middleton, we find him in Barnes London in the 1911 census as John Castle-Marsh, bookmaker born in Victoria Australia. He is with his wife Beatrice and children Mabel Frances Elsie (born around 1903) and D'arcy Gilbert (born March 1906 in London as Middleton) and employs two household servants. On January 27th 1906 Gilbert Allan Middleton married Beatrice Elizabeth Gardiner in London. On September 2nd 1908 the couple traveled from Southampton to New York on 'SS Majestic' with one of the gang convicted back in 1902. Gilbert was a "broker" on the manifest. On September 17th 1908 Beatrice was found in bed with the other gang member at the 'Majestic Hotel' in New York. Gilbert (now an automobile dealer) sued for divorce. Beatrice and Percy had left the 'Hotel Collingwood' together on September 12th. The judge refused to grant the divorce due to a technicality. Mention was made of their son D'arcy but not of Mabel Frances.

As we saw earlier, Gilbert and Beatrice were living in London with the children in 1911, and in October 1913 Gilbert sailed to New York as Gilbert Marsh with his brother. By 1918 Gilbert Marsh had settled at Epsom and co-owned "Bruce Lodge" (a horse racing establishment). In September 1920 he was suspected of involvement in a racing swindle, but was not prosecuted. Gilbert was now also described as "an affluent metal merchant" and a "contractor".

In May 1921 Gilbert Marsh was arrested at Dover, about to leave for Europe. At London's 'Old Bailey' on July

13th 1921 Marsh and other members of the gang (mostly Australian) were found guilty of obtaining large sums of money by betting and card tricks. Each man was sentenced to five years in prison and Gilbert Marsh was sent to 'Parkhurst Prison' on the Isle of Wight. By June 1925 he had been released.

In February 1923 an Australian jockey and criminal who had known Gilbert Marsh since 1919 told his story to an English newspaper. He described Gilbert as a "master crook" who was "unscrupulous" and "heartless". In 1919 he appeared to be very wealthy. He was very clever but his brother D'arcy was even more so (being shrewd and careful with the brain of a general). The jockey declared that D'arcy had gone into the room where Billie Carleton lay dead to recover the jewellery that belonged to him.

On October 7th 1921 Beatrice Marsh, her daughter (a typist) and son (a student) left England for Montreal in Canada on 'Melita'. The family remained in Canada where D'arcy was well educated and became known as a journalist, essayist and biographer in Vancouver. At one time Beatrice was a prominent dog breeder. By the time Beatrice died in Vancouver in March 1966 Mabel Frances was Mrs. Graham Gorrie of High Wycombe in England.

Gilbert Marsh was still serving his five year sentence when he was arrested at 'Parkhurst Prison' in June 1925. Gilbert Marsh "engineer" of Bruce Lodge Epsom was remanded at Bow Street Police Court for extradition on a 1921 bankruptcy warrant from Belgium. In August 1913 he had been pronounced bankrupt in Belgium but it was alleged that he had fraudulently taken away and concealed his assets. In 1912-13 Gilbert and his brother John Darlington Marsh had run an amusement park at the 'Ghent Exhibition'. Gilbert declared that both brothers had lost heavily in the venture, and that he himself had lost £70,000. When no further evidence came from Belgium, he was granted a ticket-of-leave and released on bail. There were suggestions that John Darlington Marsh had also squirreled money out of Belgium and that this had been secretly inherited by Gilbert (and concealed from his creditors) but in early August 1925 the case was dismissed due to insufficient evidence.

In late 1925 and early 1926 Gilbert Marsh was busily filing patents for inventions that included drawing instruments and devices to improve the performance of cricket and baseball bats. On April 1st 1926 he sailed for New York on 'Niew Amsterdam' as an "engineer" now living in Seaford Sussex. His nearest relative in England was listed as his sister Edith Annie Davidson (in Seaford). If she was there it was only visiting, as both Edith (1965) and her husband (1945) died in Victoria Australia. Gilbert returned to Seaford on 'Mauretania' in May 1926.

By 1928 when Gilbert Marsh engineer visited Buenos Aires in Argentina he was living in Adelphi in London. In 1931 he visited Bermuda, and in 1935 when he visited New York his home address was given as "The Old Garden" at Maresfield Park in Uckfield England. When D'arcy Gilbert Marsh married in Canada in 1940 his father "Alan Gilbert Marsh" of London was acknowledged in newspapers. When Beatrice died in Canada in 1966 newspapers stated that she had been widowed since 1942, although I cannot locate a death record for Gilbert. There is no sign of him in Epsom Cemetery with his beloved brother.

Sketch Gilbert Middleton 1902

D'arcy aka John Darlington Marsh 1917

Sarah Hershey Eddy Marsh

Ivor Tate O'Connor Marsh

Billie Carleton

Beatrice Elizabeth Marsh in old age

Godfrey Henry Egremont Gee (1844-1923)

Godfrey was born in Dorset England in 1844. His parents Thomas Egremont Gee and Mary Ann Birley had married in her hometown of Doncaster in Yorkshire in 1843. Thomas Gee's mother was Elizabeth Egremont and this middle name was incorporated into the family surname (later Godfrey was to entirely drop the Gee).

Mary Ann Birley was well educated and her father Joseph was sometime mayor and alderman of Doncaster and a grocer, confectioner and corn dealer by trade. From 1841 until 1850 Thomas Egremont Gee was living in Wimborne St Giles in Dorset and leasing farmland as a "yeoman". In 1850 Thomas, his wife and two children (Maurice Birley Egremont Gee was born in 1847) moved to Old Stratford in Warwickshire. In June 1850 Mrs. Thomas Egremont Gee was succeeding a Miss Marsh in charge of the education of young gentlemen and setting up a "Preparatory Establishment for Young Gentlemen" at 'Shakespeare Villa' in Bishopton Spa Stratford-on-Avon. The 'Birmingham Journal' of June 15th 1850 noted that Mrs. Gee had "long experience in tuition".

The 'Leamington Spa Courier' of January 3rd 1852 reported that Mrs. Egremont Gee was also establishing a school for the education of young ladies at "Old Town House" Stratford-on-Avon, but by May 22nd 1852 the family was leaving for Australia (reason unknown). They arrived in Adelaide South Australia on 'Prince Regent' on October 15th 1852. There is an 'Adelaide City Directory' listing for 1854 recording T.E. Gee as a "draper" in

Angas Street but from 1857 the family had moved to Chapel Street in Norwood. Lionel Carley Egremont Gee was born in 1854 and another son was born in 1859 but died in 1860. How Thomas financially supported his family until his death in 1862 is not clear. From June 1872 until January 1874 his widow Mary Ann (nee Birley) was again running classes for the education of young ladies at "Ribston Cottage" in Chapel Street Norwood. The cottage was sold in 1880 and Mary probably moved in with her son Lionel at Kensington Park in Adelaide (where she died in April 1897).

Godfrey Henry Egremont Gee was to become the "black sheep" of the family. His brother Maurice died in Adelaide in July 1922. An obituary in the 'Chronicle' of July 15th 1922 states that he never married, led a very quiet and retired life and was well known in musical and dramatic circles. For years he sang in a church choir at Burnside. The only brother mentioned in that obituary is Lionel. Lionel Carley Egremont Gee died in Adelaide in 1936. He had entered the civil service in 1870, married in 1879, was 'Warden of Goldfields' from 1886 until 1889 and was appointed 'Inspector of Mines and Warden' in 1896. He conducted land surveys and supervised goldfields and in 1912 was appointed 'Chief Registrar of Mines and Recorder'. He retired from the 'Mines Department' in 1924.

Godfrey Henry Egremont Gee married Irish born Mary Ellen Haynes at Norwood on February 3rd 1870. Their first child Mary Maud Egremont Gee was born "prematurely" at Norwood on September 5th 1870.

Godfrey had just been elected as Secretary to the 'Adelaide Kensington and Norwood Building and Investment Society' on November 26th 1869. Prior to that he had failed in his venture as a music seller and publisher in Adelaide. He took over the lease on 68 Rundle Street in April 1866 and the "Musical Repository" became a "Music Warehouse" and Godfrey even imported pianos. In January 1868 he was appointed music seller to the 'Duke of Edinburgh' but later that month he was declared insolvent. As a keen writer and singer of songs he was motivated to publish his own work, and he was secretary to the 'Popular Concert Committee' and a tuner and repairer of pianos. In June 1868 the stock in trade and book debts of the shop were sold, and in July 1868 the leasehold (still with four years to run) was for sale. In June 1869 the debts were settled by paying 2/3d in the pound to creditors.

Godfrey Egremont was also regarded as a "writer of vigorous prose and good verse", and once edited the 'Adelaide Punch'. In 1873 he published through a London publisher his 'Poems and Songs'. In 1892 a poem of his entitled "Democracy" was pronounced by a Boston literary expert to be "one of the greatest sonnets in the English language".

After his business failure Godfrey was lucky to obtain the position with the Building Society, but with four more children born by 1879 he probably required more income (nevertheless, Mary Ellen did employ a general servant and a boy to milk the cow). In October 1879 he advertised his "commodious house" 'Reedness' in Balliol

Street College Town as available to let during the family's visit to their summer residence at Port Elliot. The tenant who took up what he believed was a six-month lease on November 6th 1879 was Joseph Eudor Pombart, and things did not go well.

Part of the agreement was that Godfrey Egremont should have use of his bedroom and library at 'Reedness' when he needed to be back in town. By early April 1880 disputes between the two had led to Pombart's gas and water being cut off and Egremont requesting his house back. On April 27th 1880 'Presiding Magistrate' Beddome decided that there was insufficient evidence to take to trial the charge by Pombart that Egremont had shot at him on April 18th with intent to cause grievous bodily harm. The allegation was that Egremont had fired a revolver from his bedroom out into the passageway where Pombart was walking. Later newspaper articles referred to Egremont's well-known "impulsive" and "excitable" character and there was a suggestion that he may have been drinking on this occasion.

By 1882 Godfrey Egremont had developed a belief in gold mining as a way to make money quickly that was "almost fanatacism". He plunged into the 'Nest Egg Gold Mining Company' at Woodside, but with no capital to back him he took money from the 'Adelaide Kensington and Norwood Building and Investment Society' as an investment or loan on the basis that regular interest would be paid back to the Society. The 'Nest Egg' public company had failed in 1884 but was bought by a small syndicate of true believers that included Egremont.

American geologist Edward Sanger corroborated Egremont's assertion that Edward William Hitchin (Chairman of the Board of Directors of the Building Society) had approved Egremont to use Society funds to invest in the 'Nest Egg' Company soon after its formation. Hitchin was probably also part of the syndicate that took it on after it's public failure, but he died in June 1885. Even if he had approved the use of Society funds, this was still a criminal activity.

Egremont mentioned that financial reverses by 1882 led to his interest in gold mining. In March 1882 'Reedness' was advertised for sale, but apparently it did not sell and over the summers of late 1883 and 1884 it was again advertised for lease. The last mention of the family at 'Reedness' was in April 1885 when Mary Ellen was advertising for a good general servant. On September 26th 1885 the birth of son Garfield Rowland Egremont took place at Norwood, and it is probable that by then the family had sold 'Reedness'. In November 1885 a different occupant was advertising for a general servant for the commodious residence on an acre that was planted with orange trees.

On October 22nd 1885 the 'Evening Journal' (Adelaide) reported that Godfrey Egremont had been missing for some days and the Directors of the Building Society were alarmed. He had not intimated to them that he was leaving Adelaide. They broke into his office and a locksmith opened the safe that contained the Society's books and empty cashboxes. Auditors were now examining the books.

Later investigations discovered that Godfrey had left Adelaide on 'Sorata' under the name of 'De Burgh' on October 5th 1885. On October 12th 1885 Mary Ellen with her six children (including the newborn son) left Adelaide on 'John Elder' under the name of Langton. On November 25th 1885 they finally joined Godfrey in Heidelberg Germany, and police had followed her trail. Godfrey was arrested and taken to Stuttgart, then extradited back to Adelaide where he arrived on 'RMS Carthage' on April 24th 1886. His family was left stranded in Germany (probably Stuttgart) "absolutely alone and unprotected, subsisting on a small allowance subscribed by relatives" who could ill-afford the money themselves. Mary Ellen's parents were both deceased by this time. The "relatives" who helped may have been her siblings or perhaps the Egremont-Gee family.

At 'Adelaide Supreme Court' on June 3rd 1886 Godfrey Egremont pleaded guilty to embezzling £519 11s 11d from a cheque paid by a grocer to the Building Society on January 12th 1885. Five more charges were not proceeded with. He insisted that he took none of the Building Society money with him when he fled. Family travel expenses were paid from the proceeds of the sale of an interest in land (Reedness?) and the surrender of a life assurance policy. He left behind a transfer of the mining lease for the 'Lone Hand' claim at Woodside to recompense the Building Society (they considered it worthless and seized some of his furniture). On the day of his departure he had paid £412 received by him for the Building Society into its account. He was sentenced to six years with hard labour, having been in prison since

April 29th, and on June 15th 1886 he was transferred to 'Yatala Prison'.

The 'South Australian Register' of June 4th 1886 noted that Egremont had previously borne a high character and superior ability. He had a high intellect and his friends were cultured. He "made the mistake of hasting to be rich" and probably thought that he could repay the Building Society. His wife would remain in Germany "for the education of her children". His eyesight was weakened by this ordeal and he was ageing greatly. On March 22nd 1889 the 'Kapunda Herald' reported that his influential and reputable friends were trying to arrange a shortening of his sentence for the sake of his wife and children. At Yatala he had worked in the quarry before being appointed librarian after the departure of another prisoner. Nevertheless he was now described as "pale and worn ….feeble and sickly". On October 3rd 1889 he was discharged by warrant of the Governor.

A 2016 article by Alexandra Ludewig states that Godfrey Egremont and his family lived in Karlsruhe Germany from at least 1891. City directories for 1893 and 1894 show Godfrey's profession as "private income" but he was probably working as a journalist. Second daughter Ethel Lucie married in Bridgend Wales in December 1896, and was given away by her mother while her father remained in Karlsruhe. Ethel died of pneumonia while on holiday in Majorca with her husband in 1929.

In 1903 Godfrey Egremont published his book 'Verse' through a New York publisher. Youngest daughter

Aileen Evelyn Laura married an Argentinian in Devon England in August 1905. She spent most of her life in Buenos Aires where she died around 1950.

The 'Register' (Adelaide) of May 15th 1906 reported that Mary Ellen and her family were living in Karlsruhe while Godfrey was engaged in London on journalistic work. From 1908 he was listed on London Electoral Registers, but his family remained in Karlsruhe. For the 1911 census Godfrey was boarding in London and his occupation is again shown as "private means". He wrote articles for the 'Pall Mall Gazette' and other English newspapers based on his knowledge of Australia and Germany, as well as poems. Eldest son Hobart Godfrey married in Karlsruhe in December 1911, and obtained a diploma in architecture there.

When the First World War broke out both Rowland/Roland and Hobart Egremont were interned in Germany. Roland was released on a prisoner exchange after only a few months owing to ill health, and was sent to England in 1915. Hobart was not released until the end of the war. He was an architect in Berlin in 1918 and in Chile and England in the early 1920's, but by 1929 he had returned to Melbourne Australia. From 1934 until his death in 1946 he lectured in German at the 'University of Melbourne'. In January 1922 Roland was living at Burgess Hill in Sussex England and importing tea from Ceylon. He also gave lessons in German and French. As a "merchant" he returned to Adelaide on 'SS Berrima' in October 1924. He married in 1926 and settled in

Burnside South Australia as a "storekeeper". He died on a visit to Scotland in October 1950.

Third daughter Mabel Norah worked as a nurse in Luton England in 1911, married in Sussex England in 1920 and had returned to Perth Western Australia by 1925. She died in Perth in 1965. Eldest daughter Mary Maud never married. She studied art in London, Paris and Germany and traveled the world often. She lived in Burgess Hill in Sussex from around 1923 (when Roland was there) and when she died there in April 1938 she left an estate of £360 19s 11d to her (already wealthy) brother in law Charles Grenville Turbervill (widower of Ethel Lucie).

We return to Godfrey Henry Egremont and Mary Ellen (nee Haynes). She maintained a low profile and probably spent much of her time visiting her geographically dispersed adult children. Her death in 1922 was registered at Lewes (near Burgess Hill in Sussex). Godfrey's last address was 205 Gray's Inn Road South St. Pancras in London. He died on March 3rd 1923 leaving an estate of £352 10s to unmarried daughter Mary Maud Egremont. Despite his character flaws and criminal lapse, Godfrey was not a bad man and he and Mary Ellen must be commended for successfully raising six children from a precarious beginning at Karlsruhe.

Yatala Prison Adelaide 1886-1889

Parents Thomas Egremont Gee and Mary Ann Birley

Godfrey Egremont Gee on left 1866 with the Clisbys outside his new music shop Rundle Street Adelaide

Lionel Carley Egremont Gee outside old family home at Norwood (1857-1880) photo taken by Mary Maud Egremont in 1927

Sebastian George (1864-1933)

Sebastian was the third son of Abraham George and Sarah (Sally) Trewartha, born in Wakefield South Australia on January 15th 1864. When the "well known and deeply respected" Abraham died of cardiac disease at his residence near Quorn in South Australia in July 1890, he left a widow and nine children to mourn his loss.

An article about Abraham George in the 'Adelaide Observer' of July 12th 1890 gives us an outline of his life. He came from Cornwall in England to Australia as a young man and was by profession "a mining and civil engineer". He had seen "many vicissitudes of fortune" and "no less than three times gained a position of fair affluence, being a victim to mining ventures, fire, and drought in succession". He was among the first colonists to travel from South Australia to the Victorian gold rush, but returned to South Australia to farm and raise sheep at Auburn "with the doubtful success generally attending upon settlers in the Northern Areas". Up to the last week of his life he was a correspondent to the 'Register' newspaper.

These vicissitudes in wealth must have made an impact upon young Sebastian, who quickly became the "black sheep" of the family in his search for fame and fortune. He was first mentioned in newspapers in October 1883 when he was assaulted with a whip in a fight with an old enemy, whilst riding with family to chapel. In early August 1884 he was writing poetry and sending it to the local paper. On August 21st 1884 he came into prominence when he gave an exposition of “mind and muscle reading” to the ‘Young Men’s Christian Association” at Port Pirie. He had lately been giving private séances, and was reportedly very successful when put to severe tests of his skill as a mind reader. Still a farmer at home in Auburn, he found ladies to be his “most sensitive and sympathetic subjects”. He was now a cousin, nephew or indeterminate relative of the famous American economist Henry George, who had published his book ‘Progress and Poverty’ in 1879. I fail to find any relationship here. Henry was born in Pennsylvania, and his father also was born in America. Sebastian’s father Abraham was born in Cornwall in England, as was Abraham’s father. Nevertheless, Sebastian throughout the rest of his life claimed kinship to Henry George, a founder of the single-tax movement.

Having found the notoriety he craved, Sebastian George continued to give mind-reading displays and conduct séances, as well as writing poetry, throughout 1885. His exploits even appeared in overseas newspapers. On September 21st 1885 South Australian newspapers reported that he was to give up mind reading for body healing. He was sailing to England on ‘Garonne’ that very day to study medicine. He had enrolled as a theological student at the ‘Bible Christian College’ in Shebbear in Devonshire, and would then study medicine at an English University.

By November 1885 English and Australian papers were reporting that Sebastian George was “astonishing Cornish people” with his thought reading powers. He was still writing stories and poems. In early October 1886 he advised South Australians in a letter that he had completed at term at 'Shebbear College' and contemplated a tour of America. On October 23rd 1886 the 'News' of Newport, Pennsylvania reported that Sebastian was to perform his "miraculous feats" of mind reading at 'Centennial Hall' in Newport with rates of admission 15 cents and 25 cents. By his own admission he had "displayed his unusual gift before the crowned heads of Europe" and he now added "De Lorne" to his name. In court in Sydney in January 1928 he declared that his mother came from a titled family by the name of D'Lorne. This is complete nonsense, as his mother Sarah/Sally Trewartha was born in Cornwall and in 1841 when she was still living with her family in Gwennap her father Sebastian was a miner.

In December 1886 Sebastian George was writing to South Australia from New York, stating that he was studying for a medical diploma. In January 1887 he wrote to the 'Boston Herald' describing his "remarkable gift" as an amateur mind reader, and the article was copied in many American papers. He also wrote from Boston to the 'South Australian Register' that he had been traveling through England and America, had met Lily Langtry and seen President Cleveland who sent him a note. He described in great detail visiting his famous "cousin" Henry George and family at their home in New York. He knew that Henry's wife was born in Sydney so perhaps he really did meet the family.

On December 14th 1888 "Dr. Sebastian de L. George" arrived in Sydney from San Francisco on 'Alameda'. He arrived back in Adelaide from Melbourne on 'Victorian' on December 20th, and the Adelaide 'Evening Journal' of December 22nd relayed his intentions. He now intended to remain in the colony and practice as a doctor, having "settled down in Chicago to the study of medicine" for two years and obtained his diploma as a Doctor of Medicine. He had also occupied himself with literary contributions to leading New York and Chicago newspapers and developed his gift of thought reading. He had declined tempting offers to remain in America giving séances. The 'Kapunda Herald' of December 25th 1888 described George as a "cute, go-ahead fellow".

With his fake medical qualifications seemingly unquestioned in Australia, Sebastian nevertheless did not take up practice as a doctor. On January 15th 1889 newspapers reported that the "well known journalist and mind reader" had taken up residence in Broken Hill in New South Wales and accepted the position of sub-editor for the 'Silver Age'. Some five years prior he had visited and foretold that Broken Hill would have a bright mining future. He intended to make his home there, but spent much of his time in Adelaide and by May 15th had located his head office there to supply the 'Barrier Miner' in Broken Hill with mining intelligence. He was now a member of the recently established 'Intercolonial Mining Intelligence Company'. On May 8th 1889 he gave an exhibition of his mind reading powers in the Institute Hall at Port Broughton in South Australia. In July 1889 he gave a similar exhibition at Silverton near Broken Hill.

Now a mining expert, in August 1889 Sebastian was appointed as Secretary to the 'Barrier Ranges Smelting Fund' at Broken Hill, a group wishing to finance the erection of smelters for Barrier mines. In December the "genial gentleman of bonhomie qualities" paid a short visit to Port Augusta. In January 1890 he gave a free public exhibition of mind reading in Williamstown Victoria at the invitation of the local Member of Parliament, and also gave private mind reading entertainments. Perhaps he met his future wife at this time.

On July 8th 1890 the 'Barrier Miner' reproduced a sarcastic sketch of Sebastian George published on May 5th 1890 in the 'New York Police Gazette'. I have no idea why American authorities were still interested in him. Amongst his self-reported achievements were – becoming a novelist at the age of ten and editor at nineteen, acting as president of a University Athletic Club in England, teaching private classes in athletics in Boston, achieving a sprint record for running 100 yards, earning seven medals for saving lives, owning several good horses and having been feted by royalty in various countries for his mind reading. He was known for his generosity to beggars and the unfortunate.

In July 1890 Sebastian's father died in rural South Australia, and on December 15th 1890 Sebastian De Lorne George married Victorian-born Violet Mabel

Frances Power in Adelaide. I cannot find any mention of the marriage in newspapers. Of three children born to the couple, only daughter Violet Myrtle George (born in Broken Hill in 1891) survived to adulthood. Two sons, both named Sebastian De Lorne George, were born in Victoria in 1892 and 1895. They died in Victoria in 1892 and Coolgardie Western Australia in 1896.

Throughout 1891 Sebastian De Lorne George was heavily involved with mining and the 'Intercolonial Mining Intelligence Company'. He began to accumulate mining leases in the Yancowinna area of New South Wales until late March 1892, when for a few years he settled in Victoria as manager of the 'Braybrook Implement Company' at Boort. In August 1895 he left Melbourne on 'Innamincka' and by late September 1895 he was in Coolgardie in Western Australia.

Still renowned as a mind reader, in February 1896 Sebastian was appointed as Secretary to the ' Goldfields Electoral Registration Leage' in Coolgardie. By April he was superintendent of the local fire brigade. By June he was master of ceremonies at a local athletic carnival, and in July he was "proud to be a naturalized American" (no evidence of this). In August he was timekeeper for a local boxing match and he successfully sold the 'Golden Ripple Mine' to an English syndicate. Throughout the following years he continued his active involvement in mining (as a "mining engineer") as well as athletics, boxing, the fire brigade and life saving. In August 1897 he was appointed to represent the working miners of Coolgardie at a Royal Commission on Mining Laws in

Western Australia. The only reference to his family was the occasional description of his wife's outfit at a local function. By late 1897 there were rumblings of discontent about the veracity of Sebastian's mining qualifications, and some of his dealings were questioned in court. By November 1898 he was described as an "auctioneer" of Coolgardie. He attempted unsuccessfully to stand for the municipal council and 'Clare's Weekly' of November 26th 1898 declared disparagingly that he was "always a grafter".

In March 1899 Sebastian George seems to have run an illegal hotel business from his home in Coolgardie. He denied this in court when he was accused of violating the 'Early Closing Act' on February 13th, and the magistrate declined to impose a fine or inflict costs. In January 1900 there was again mention of his "shop" and an intoxicated man outside it. Still an "auctioneer", he nominated again in November 1899 for the municipal elections.

The 'Sun' (Kalgoorlie) of November 11th 1900 stated that "those who know George would take no notice of anything he might say". It seems that his reputation in Coolgardie was rapidly declining, and probably for this reason he left for an appointment as "Resident Magistrate and Resident Medical Officer" at Broome in Western Australia in early April 1901. There was immediate political outcry over the appointment. According to the 'Murchison Times and Day Dawn Gazette' of April 2nd 1901 George had "commenced life as an iron founder, drifted into the marine store business and finally evolved into a thought reader at so much per head". His medical qualifications were questioned, and Sebastian George retreated from Broome in haste.

On December 20th 1902 the 'Kalgoorlie Miner' reported that Sebastian George was one of many Australians now in Johannesburg in South Africa, and that he was "in rather a big way of business". The 'Sunday Press' of April 12th 1903 included Mr. H.S. de L. George amongst "Australian hustlers" in Johannesburg. He was signing himself "late engineer to the Mines Department and Royal Commission on Mining in Western Australia", but "was ever a perverse and incorrigible liar" who never held the position of engineer with the Mines Department. "His stock in trade consisted of brazen impudence and the rankest inexperience." He was currently floating the 'Rose Mount G.M. Syndicate Limited' in Johannesburg.

In December 1904 a Tasmanian newspaper reported that Mr. Sebastian De Lorne George was "President of the Australian Association of the Rand and a Justice of the Peace" in Johannesburg. On May 15th 1906 he was fined £5 for assault in Johannesburg (details unknown) and his fingerprints were taken. On December 13th 1906 the 'Register' (Adelaide) published a letter from Sebastian George in Johannesburg, in which he foretold a great future for South Australian diamonds and declared that his speculations in Transvaal diamond and gold mines were paying well. He was proposing a return to his homeland if his acquired knowledge about diamonds "could be made use of" there.

On April 27th 1907 in Pretoria South Africa George was found guilty of mining fraud and sentenced to 15 months in prison. This time his fingerprints were not recorded. On August 26th 1908 he was deported from South Africa and he arrived in Sydney on 'Miltiades' from Capetown in September 1908. On September 19th 1908 Violet Mabel Frances George and her daughter Violet Myrtle (an artist on the ship's manifest) arrived in London on 'Geelong' from Durban.

By late October 1908 Sebastian George was back in Broken Hill looking for mines (especially bismuth) for a Sydney-based company 'International Mines Limited'. He also restarted the 'Tara Mine' at Mount Gipps and was staying at the 'Freemasons Hotel' in Broken Hill. He was writing for the 'Register' in Adelaide saying that he was a duly qualified mining engineer and had been 'Inspector of Mines' in Johannesburg. By December he was back to giving mind reading exhibitions in Broken Hill, timekeeping for boxing matches and floating tin mines.

On March 30th 1909 Violet Mabel Frances and Violet Myrtle George arrived back in Brisbane from London on 'Marathon'. They rejoined Sebastian and the family settled back in Adelaide, where he gave lectures on "mental photography" and led a new 'Boys Brigade' group. He continued his mining interests in coal and mercury and by October 1911 was "doing well" in Adelaide. In 1912 he branched into radium, gold, copper and petroleum. Living at Hyde Park in Adelaide, Violet Mabel Frances was sued in August 1912 by a piano warehouse when the promissory note she had used to pay for a piano was dishonoured by the bank.

On December 29th 1913 Violet Myrtle George (only daughter of Mr. and Mrs. S. de L. George of Francis Street Hyde Park) married Joseph Jesse Barrett and the marriage was announced in papers in January 1914. Barrett had arrived from South Africa on 'Runic' in July 1912 and had previously visited Adelaide as a prominent cricketer. In Durban he was chief buyer for a timber importer and he now secured a responsible position with a leading Adelaide firm. Both he and Violet Myrtle were popular and the wedding was a large one.

After their wedding the Barretts seem to have lived at Francis Street with the Georges. In April 1916 and January 1918 Sebastian and his wife were still attending affairs and traveling together. In June 1917 Mr. S. George and Mrs. J.J. Barrett of Hyde Park entertained friends. In late March 1919 Dr. Henry Sebastian De Lorne George was sent by the Adelaide 'Central Board of Health' to Port Pirie to take charge of the 'Isolation Hospital' during an influenza epidemic. Authorities apparently recognized his brief medical appointment to Broome in 1901 as sufficient evidence that he was properly qualified. George had applied for a military commission hoping to get away to the war but was instead appointed to the 'Australian Army Medical Corps Reserve' on July 25th 1918.

By the end of April 1919 the epidemic at Port Pirie was "flickering out" and George's work was completed.

Relations between George and the 'Port Pirie Local Board of Health' had not been cordial. The 'Recorder' of May 27th 1919 declared that the "well-known mining expert and company promoter" was not a medical man. He gave British qualifications but was not on the register of the 'British Medical Association'. His association with the 'Army Medical Corps' had now been terminated, and he was charged with racking up a huge wine bill in Port Pirie. In a long letter of reply to the 'Recorder' George signed himself as "Surgeon Captain".

Another article in the 'Recorder' on May 25th 1929 gave more detail about this period. Sebastian George had insisted upon being supplied with large quantities of 'Chateau Tanunda' brandy (he bathed his patients in it! and drank it himself with peppermint as an antidote to the flu). His domestic staff at the 'Isolation Hospital' included a chef. The 'Recorder' of April 12th 1954 adds that he ordered to be brought from Adelaide to Port Pirie a motor vehicle that "proved useless for ambulance work but was fine for joy riding".

On January 30th 1921 Violet Myrtle Barrett died at the age of twenty-nine. While Violet Mabel Frances possibly remained with Joseph Jesse Barrett in Francis Street Hyde Park, in August 1921 Sebastian George was reportedly living in Glenelg. There was still interaction between the pair. In December 1921 Mr. and Mrs. George were presented with a handsome salad service for their work with an Adelaide dog club. In February 1923 a newspaper memorial notice for the death of Myrtle Barrett came only from Violet, with no mention of

Sebastian. In August 1923 there was mention of Mrs. George visiting her husband's office (he was a "Mining Engineer" and "Mining Company Secretary") in North Terrace in Adelaide.

In September 1923 Sebastian advertised for a managing partner to take a half share in his business. It had a large clientele, substantial property, thousands of shares and large interests in mines. He was making the sacrifice on account of ill health. He was moving his head office from Adelaide to Sydney, and the assets he advertised for sale included household furniture. The move to Sydney amounted to the desertion of his wife. On August 11th 1924 Sebastian was before a court in Sydney for wife desertion, and was ordered to pay just under £50 to Violet Mabel Frances. This was still unpaid in November 1924.

On October 20th 1924 the 'Evening News' (Sydney) reported that Dr. Henry George was one of two men accused at the Central Court of conspiracy to cheat and defraud Dr. David Morrison of large sums of money. George was living in a flat at Cremorne, and acting as a broker for the 'Australian Medical and General Insurance Association' of Sydney (described as a "Wild Cat" firm). Morrison was recently arrived in the city and looking for work, and was told by George that he personally knew Lord Kitchener and Sir Douglas Haig. Morrison was inveigled to buy £250 of worthless shares in the Association, but had only paid £125 and given a promissory note for the balance. Of this George received £50 and his co-accused £75. At the Sydney Quarter

Sessions on November 10th 1924 both accused were found guilty and remanded for sentence.

Four days later at Darlinghurst Court George, whose history had now come to light but who had lied about his age, was bound over on a personal recognizance of £100 and a surety. His New South Wales gaol record states that he was born in Ireland in 1854, and nobody thought to check the validity. The judge decided he would not send George to gaol because of his age. He could pay £50 to be released from Long Bay Gaol and that amount was owed on an order for wife maintenance. His co-accused was forced to pay the whole £125 in restitution to Dr. David Morrison. George again lied about his medical qualifications, but could not name the university at which he had taken his medical degree. He admitted to the assault charge in 1906 because his fingerprints matched, but not to the 1907 fraud in Pretoria because there were no fingerprints from that. He was a retired captain of the 'Army Medical Corps', had been a doctor on several ships and practiced at Port Pirie and Broken Hill.

On June 8th 1926 Violet Mabel Frances George (nee Power) died at the residence of her son-in-law Joseph Jesse Barrett in Kingswood Adelaide. A newspaper obituary mentioned that with her daughter she had spent some years in South Africa and made a trip to England prior to returning to Australia. She had lived with Barrett for about fourteen years and her only living sister Emily Davey was the wife of the Burra Town Clerk. Her husband and his misdemeanors were not mentioned.

For a time Sebastian George had returned to mining activities after his escape from gaol, but in December 1927 he was arrested for practicing as a medical man at Wiseman's Ferry in September and October of that year. Still living in Cremorne, he had gained a position as a first aid officer with the 'Mains Road Board' at Wiseman's Ferry and in that capacity had issued illegal medical certificates signed with false qualifications. In court Henry Sebastian De Lorne George was described as a "well groomed elderly man". The case was heard at Windsor Court on January 23rd 1928. George said his mother came from a titled family by the name of D'Lorne and that he was a personal friend of the late King Edward VII and of every crown head in Europe as well as the King of Honolulu. The prosecution case fell apart because George had been accepted as a doctor (erroneously) by the Adelaide 'Central Board of Health' back in 1919, and by the 'Army Medical Corps Reserve' in 1918. One newspaper sarcastically remarked that "the army can do no wrong".

In May 1929 an old resident of Port Pirie reminisced in the 'Recorder' about Sebastian George in 1919. He had a "magnetic personality" and seemed "able to calm and soothe" hospital patients possibly by a hypnotic influence. He had set the whole town drinking "Chateau and Pep" during his stay at Port Pirie, and was a real autocrat.

On Wednesday May 20th 1931 Dr. Henry George of Cremorne was charged at Central Police Court in Sydney with having assaulted a ferry ticket examiner after he had refused to allow him through the quay barrier without a ticket. Still lying about his age (giving 77) he said he was ill and had a bad memory. He was fined for fare evasion and the assault.

At Central Police Court on October 8th 1931 Dr. Henry Sebastian George was initially fined £250 (in default 500 days gaol) for being in possession of cocaine while not a registered medical practitioner. He said his skull was fractured while serving as Surgeon-Captain with the 'Black Watch' in a war in the Sudan resulting in a loss of memory. He was entitled to buy cocaine as an ex-Surgeon Major of the Canadian Mounted Police. A police sergeant testified that George was eccentric and a reputed abortionist. The judge reduced his fine to £10 (in default 20 days gaol). George was described as having an "upright figure", "alert carriage" and "jet black moustache and hair".

On September 7th 1933 Sebastian George died in 'Sydney Hospital' after a short illness. An obituary for Mr. S. George in the 'Sydney Morning Herald' of September 11th stated that he was the son of Abraham George and cousin of Henry George the single-taxer. He took an active part in the opening up of mines in Broken Hill and later went to the Kimberley goldfields in South Africa and floated several companies there. His wife had died ten years ago. There was no mention of his fraudulent medical activities. A shorter version of the article appeared in the Melbourne 'Herald'. His funeral was held at the Methodist portion of the Northern Suburbs

Cemetery and he has a designated grave there under "S.H. George".

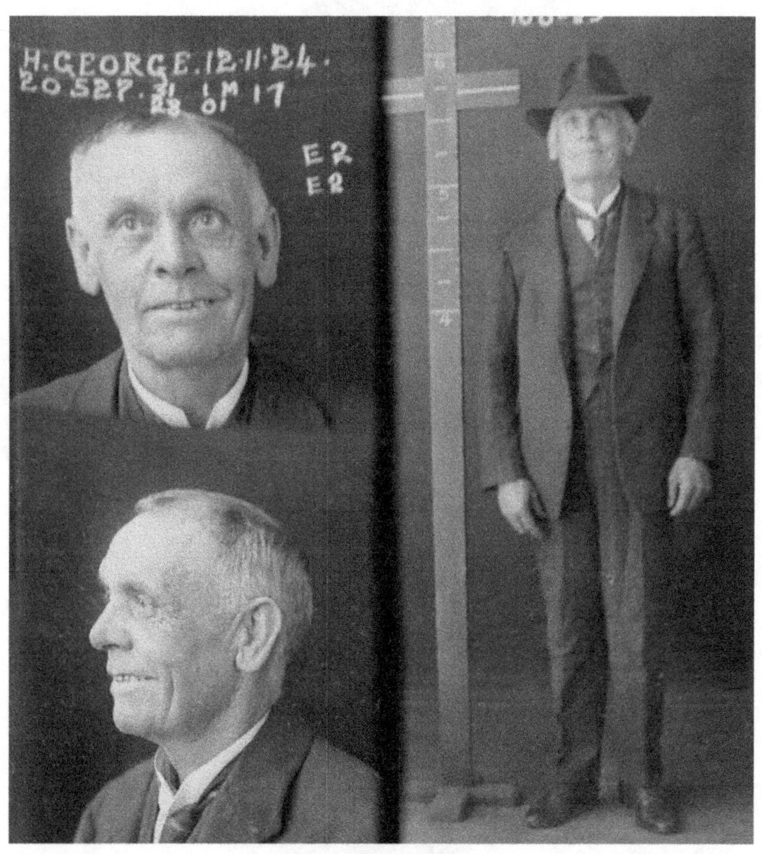

Sebastian George Sydney November 1924 (height 5'8½")

Sarah/Sally George (nee Trewartha)

Tombstone Payneham Cemetery Sebastian's daughter and wife

Thomas Patrick Kavanagh (1843-1890)

Kavanagh was born in Victoria, Australia to Irish immigrants James Patrick Kavanagh and Margaret Freeman Horan. Margaret died at Springfield near Essendon in June 1859 and James died at Springfield in April 1860. He left an estate valued at around £600 to be administered by his two brothers, to be divided between his three sons and two daughters. In August 1861 Thomas Patrick Kavanagh purchased 'Cambo Cambo Station' near Glenelg for £18,000. In February 1862 he was described as "Thomas P. Kavanagh of Springfield near Melbourne and Cambo Cambo Station" and his sheep bore the brand "TPK".

On April 30th 1862 Thomas Patrick Kavanagh of Melbourne married Kate Gates (daughter of Geelong grocer James Gates) at St Francis' Cathedral in Melbourne. On August 28th 1862, that part of his father's land at Springfield which had been inherited by Thomas was sold by order of the Sheriff. This followed litigation by John Hussey, and no doubt Kavanagh was in debt to the plaintiff and living beyond his means. I cannot find any further mention of 'Cambo Cambo Station'.

In October and November 1863 Thomas Patrick Kavanagh was sued by one Elizabeth Bradley for wages owed to her by him. The defendant did not appear at Essendon Police Court and disappeared. In February 1864 he was arrested by Richmond Police and dealt with under the Vagrants Act after obtaining a suspension of Bradley's warrant through false pretenses. He was found at the house of James Levack on February 16th 1864. In March 1864 at Essendon Police Court Thomas Patrick Kavanagh was summoned by Susan Bailey for refusing to maintain his illegitimate five month old child. She had known him for two years, and he had paid £1 per week to her until a month earlier when he said he was tired of her and wanted a change. He had repeatedly promised to marry her and kept her in Collingwood, and she believed he was now married. The only child born to a Susan Bailey during this period was at Collingwood in 1864, with the father listed as Richard Brooks.

After their marriage in 1862, a son named James Freeman Kavanagh was born to Thomas and Kate in 1865, but he died at eleven days of age. The birth of another son with the same name was recorded in 1867 but if this was correct he presumably also died as a baby, and nothing more is known of him.

From early September 1866 Thomas Patrick Kavanagh worked for a firm at 51 Temple Court in Melbourne, as an agent selling Allen's ointment for foot rot and scab. A successful salesman for the product, by early 1869 he was working for Gideon Lang at 35 Queen Street Melbourne. In March 1869 Kavanagh and John Van Hemert paid £4,000 for the sole right to sell the Allen's product. The partnership was dissolved by mutual consent in June 1869, and Thomas Patrick Kavanagh would carry on the business alone.

As a commercial traveler for his company, Kavanagh was arrested in Sydney in August 1869 on a warrant for obtaining money by false pretenses issued at Queanbeyan. Calling himself Michael Cavanagh (but stating that he worked for his actual Melbourne firm) he had stayed at an inn belonging to Henry Cane and paid his bill with a cheque that was subsequently dishonoured. He was described as around 5'6"-5'7" in height, of stout build with brown hair and sandy whiskers, with a smart respectable appearance and he spoke "very quietly". He was granted bail and would stand trial at Queanbeyan on October 4th. On September 23rd 1869 the Attorney General declined to prosecute the case.

In February 1870 the firm of "T.P. Kavanagh & Co" was still operating from 35 Queen Street in Melbourne selling its Allen's ointment. The family residence was listed in the Melbourne 'Sand's Directory' at 27 Peel Street Hotham. On December 16th 1870 a warrant was issued against Thomas Patrick Kavanagh for deserting his child at Hotham in March. It was believed that he was in Sydney as agent for Allen's foot rot ointment. A son named Albert Henry Kavanagh was born to Thomas and Kate in 1870, and buried in Melbourne General Cemetery at Carlton with his Kavanagh grandparents on October 16th 1870. Although Victorian death records indicate that the child was around five months old, it is almost certain that Albert was the child deserted in March.

On October 20th 1871 Thomas Patrick Kavanagh (still in Sydney) disobeyed an order of the court for maintenance of his wife for £3 per week. The order had been made a few weeks earlier and the money was now paid. There was no mention of a child. Kate was now in Sydney also, and in September 1871 she was staying at 'Windsor House' in Jamison Street Sydney when she was trying to contact her cousin James M. Gates. She probably then returned to her hometown of Geelong (where both her parents still lived). On June 22nd 1872 the ‘New South Wales Police Gazette' reported that Kavanagh was said to be residing at 'Cohen's Hotel' at Wynyard Square in Sydney. He was still an agent for Allen’s foot-rot ointment and it was believed that his wife had left Geelong about three months earlier with the intention of going to him. On September 18th 1872 Kavanagh was charged at Central Police Court in Sydney by his wife Kate with desertion and leaving her without means of support. Thomas was ordered to pay her forty shillings per week plus court costs and a surety of £100 to ensure his compliance. Kate no doubt returned to Geelong.

On March 27th 1871, a solicitor named W. Matson of Wynyard Square Sydney advertised for any just claims against T.F.P Kavenagh late of Port Augusta and Marachowie to be sent to him as the Melbourne firm was to be liquidated. This year is the first in which Thomas Patrick Kavanagh decided to add ‘F’ (for Frank) to his name, possibly after encountering a Brisbane man with that name.

By October 1872 Thomas Patrick Frank Kavanagh (with variations) had become friendly with businessman Charlton James Park and his wife. When the ‘Long Drive Gold Mining Company' was registered in October 1872 Charlton Park of 50 Margaret Street Sydney bought 200 shares and Frank P. Kavanagh of 13 Barrack Street

Sydney bought 25 shares. In June 1873 Charlton Park was in London as an officer of the 'Liverpool and London Globe Insurance Company' when he wrote a letter to the editor of the 'Australasian' about Lincolnshire sheep. In the letter he mentioned that a gentleman named Mr. T.F.P. Kavenagh from New South Wales was taking sheep to Melbourne.

When the 'Great Australian Gold Mining Company' was registered in February 1873, Thomas Frank Patrick Kavanagh became its "Managing Director" in Sydney. He was now a "Barrister at Law". In May 1874 Charlton James Park ("a gentleman of eminent standing in Sydney") became a Director. On May 13th 1874 a man named Walter alleged that Kavanagh was indebted to him and was about to leave the colony. The defendant denied both assertions, and with affidavits from powerful friends he was believed. In December 1874 Charlton Park, gentleman of Pitt Street Sydney, became insolvent.

Despite high profile directors in London and Sydney, on May 24th 1875 the future of the 'Great Australian Gold Mining Company' was being assessed at a committee meeting. The 'Sydney Morning Herald' of October 26th 1875 stated that Kavanagh had become a bankrupt since the May meeting (which I cannot verify) and that he had opted to take fully paid up shares in the company in lieu of cash. Kavanagh and other vendors had painted the prospects too brightly but would not be charged with fraud. Kavanagh had effectively resigned as Secretary "by quitting the colony", leaving no instructions. The committee recommended winding up the company.

Because of his close association with Thomas Patrick Kavanagh, Charlton James Park was a ruined man in every way. Evidence given at an unrelated (Dibbs) divorce case in 1880 stated that in January 1874 the Park family and Kavanagh all lived at 'Wentworth House' (a boarding house) in Wynyard Square. When the Park family went to Cook's River in that same year, Kavanagh was there too, and he appeared to have no home of his own. Charlton Park had married Alice Rosa Bremer in October 1863. A daughter (Nina Isabel) was born on August 11th 1864 and son (Charlton Albert) was born in 1866.

Despite his protestations in May 1874 that he had no intentions of leaving the colony, Kavanagh (barrister) arrived in London on December 21st 1874. He was staying at the 'Bedford Hotel' in Covent Garden and briefly got into trouble when he tendered an Australian half-sovereign at the 'Black Swan Hotel'. The 'Daily Telegraph' of December 8th 1880 reported that Kavanagh and the Park family had all gone to England together, and that Mrs. Park returned from England with Kavanagh and without her husband. Whether Charlton Senior did accompany his family or not, it is certain that on February 19th 1877 Alice Parks, her two children and Frank Kavanagh (lawyer) arrived in New York from London on 'Utopia'.

The fate of Charlton James Park is tragic. On June 12th 1880 he was arrested in the vicinity of South Grafton and charged with lunacy. Described as "the husband of Mrs. Park in the Dibbs case", he had inflicted wounds on himself with a knife. After his 1874 insolvency, Park had probably moved to the Clarence region of New South Wales by October 1876. Despite his setbacks, he took up a "pretty large" selection at Corinda near the sea about fifty miles south of Grafton. This "man of education and culture" who was at one time Secretary of the 'Australian Mutual Provident Society' took a prominent part in the public matters of his new district until his death on January 8th 1893.

One of the London Directors of the 'Great Australian Gold Mining Company' was General Erskine Hicks. Now in London at the end of 1874, Kavanagh and Hicks along with two other men formed the 'Percy and Kelly Nickel, Cobalt and Chrome Iron Mining Company Limited' and opened it up to public subscription. The prospects of the company mine in Noumea were spruiked, but it was not successful and on April 29th 1876 the Secretary (who had not received his promised salary) petitioned to wind up the company. Creditors were asked to send particulars of their claims to the official liquidator by October 2nd 1876. In June and July 1877 a gentleman living in Paris sued several directors for obtaining money from him for subscriptions under false pretenses. At Bow Street Police Court in London, the company was described as "sham". Kavanagh had fled to New York in February and General Erskine Hicks (company chairman) also failed to appear. Kavanagh had attended board meetings in London and Paris as an agent for the vendors. He provided letters to prosecutor Montagu Williams that showed Hicks and other directors in a bad light, and it was suggested that Kavanagh might be more useful as a witness than a defendant. General Hicks died in France in February 1880. The other two men charged with fraud were both acquitted in October 1877.

Alleged barrister Frank Kavanagh now turned his fraudulent attentions towards his new home in New York. By June 1st 1877 he had been a judge at a recent dog show and declared that he was a relative of the armless and legless Britism M.P. Arthur MacMurrough Kavanagh. The 'Evening News' (Sydney) of June 15th 1881, in its long article about "Champagne Frank" declared that by the time Kavanagh arrived in Chicago word was received from that illustrious parliamentarian that he did not know this "Frank" and he suspected he had traded upon his name also in Australia. At the 'Westminster Kennel Club' dog show in New York Kavanagh was accompanied by his "cousin" Mrs. Alice Parks of Sydney and a valuable fox terrier. Now in high favour with the elite of New York, Frank Kavanagh set up and promoted the 'Manhattan Cab Company Limited' and pledged to buy 1,500 shares at $100 each when the books opened. He also promised to obtain capital from England for the venture. Alice Parks reportedly assisted by courting several leading American insurance companies to become involved.

By late September 1877 there were no cabs or even promises of cabs, and Kavanagh was in Philadelphia raising capital and reportedly "sanguine of ultimate success". By October 6th 1877 the cheap cab scheme in New York had failed and proprietor Frank Kavanagh had not put up a sliver of the promised English capital. On

October 13th 1877 a committee of commissioners met and voted to dissolve the company. It was noted that Kavanagh "lived very extravagantly". He had purportedly taken money by promising people jobs in the company, borrowed from people who were not repaid, cashed a dishonoured draft with the 'First National Bank' and created fictitious authorizations from Lord Roseberry and others. Charges would be presented against him.

The next we hear of Frank Kavanagh "described as a barrister but not in the English law list" is in October 1879 in Manchester England. He was charged with having obtained goods by false pretences, but the jury could not agree and he was retried in December. This time he was found guilty and sentenced to five months with hard labour.

At Manchester City Police Court on December 16th 1880 the "smart looking man" Frank T. McMurrough Kavanagh (said to be a barrister in Australia), English solicitor's clerk Edward Firth and Alice Park were remanded on several charges of conspiring to defraud tradesmen out of their goods in Manchester and Salford. They had obtained furniture on May 24th that was delivered to Kavanagh's house at 35 Carter Street Greenheys, and jewellery and clothing. Kavanagh said that he worked in Gorton and he produced letter paper stamped with 'Kavanagh and Company, fire extinguisher manufacturers' but there was no such business. The accused were later also charged with selling milk adulterated with water. In November 1880 Kavanagh told a tailor he had been Postmaster General in Australia and to a jeweler he stated that he was connected with a London banking firm. The "respectably-dressed" Alice Park lived with Kavanagh as his wife. When the accused were committed for trial on February 10th 1881, she fainted in court.

At the Manchester Quarter Sessions on February 19th 1881 all three accused were found guilty. Alice Park and Edward Firth were sentenced to 12 months prison with hard labour, Kavanagh to five years. The 'Manchester Times' noted that magistrate Leresche described Park as "a member of a good family, but since coming under the influence of Kavanagh she had aided him in his system of swindling". Indeed, Alice Rosa Bremer was the granddaughter of Rear-Admiral Sir J.J. Gordon Bremer K.C.B. of Devon and her father served as collector of customs in Sydney.

For the 1881 English census we find Alice Park (factory worker) in Gorton Prison, Lancashire. Her children were boarding at Chorlton on Medlock in Manchester and Charles Albert Park was working as an office boy. Frank Thomas Cavanagh (barrister born in Ireland) was in Millbank prison in London. The much younger Edward Firth (articled clerk born in Leeds) was in Gorton prison.

On April 5th 1886 at London's 'Old Bailey' Thomas Frank Patrick Kavanagh (barrister) pleaded guilty to obtaining goods such as cutlery, cigars and wines to the value of around £300-£400 from tradesmen by false pretenses in London. Trial records show that he was still attempting to sell his Compound Automatic Fire

Extinguisher under 'Kavanagh, Cooke and Company". He seems to have been living alone, renting a room in Duke Street Adelphi from March 1885. He may have still been in contact with Alice Park and her children in London (Nina Isabel Park married in Poplar in London on September 24th 1887). Kavanagh was sentenced to five years prison.

On January 27th 1887 Thomas Frank Patrick Kavanagh was sent from Dartmoor to Portsea Island Prison. From January 17th 1889 he was a patient at the prison infirmary suffering from lung disease and neuralgic pain. During his prison service he was employed as a baker. He died at the prison on April 12th 1890 from natural causes (peritonitis ensuing from erysipelas). The death was registered under the name of Thomas Frank Kavanagh and he lies in Kingston Cemetery.

The legitimate wife of Thomas Patrick Kavanagh, Kate Gates, married confectioner Thomas Riggs in Sydney on August 3rd 1893. Riggs had just moved up from Melbourne and probably met Kate in Victoria. She describes herself as a widow (did she know Kavanagh had died?) and the daughter of deceased Geelong grocer James Gates. Thomas Riggs, his mother and brother all settled in Newtown in Sydney after the suicide of his father (a retired police sergeant and latterly Collingwood grocer) in January 1894 in Victoria (after a domestic quarrel). Kate Riggs died on August 11th 1929, when the couple was living at Crows Nest. Thomas Riggs moved to Waverley where he died on June 2nd 1932. Both lie in the Northern Suburbs Cemetery.

Around 1889 Nina Isabel Park and her new husband Charles Alfred Percy Gardiner (a seaman) arrived in Honolulu accompanied by Alice Park, who took on a new identity as Alice Maclean. A daughter named Nina Gardiner was born in Woollahra in Sydney in 1889, and the family probably arrived in Honolulu on 'Hayward' from Sydney on October 18th 1889. Percy deserted his wife in Honolulu around 1893 and went to San Francisco. In December 1895 Nina Gardiner arrived in Sydney from Honolulu and accused her husband of desertion and bigamy (he married another woman in Sydney in January 1895). Percy declared to police that he thought his wife "got a divorce in Honolulu".

Back in Honolulu, Nina Isabel Gardiner married Henry William Flint (a police captain) on January 4th 1899, but the marriage was short-lived. By 1910 Nina Isabel had reverted to the surname Gardiner and was living with her mother Alice Maclean and daughter Nina Gardiner, and a lodger. Alice remained living with her daughter in Honolulu until her death as Alice Rosa Park on November 19th 1921. In June 1907 Charlton Alfred Park made a visit to his mother and sister from Sydney.

The 'Honolulu Star Bulletin' of November 21st 1921 explains why this "Englishwoman" had lived under an assumed name for thirty-two years until her death. It was "because of grief at the death of her loved ones in England". The story of Mrs. Charlton James Park only became known as her funeral was taking place. Her late husband was a son of an English J.P. Her brother was the late Commander James Gordon Bremer. She had a long list of relatives among members of the British Peerage. She was survived by her daughter Nina Gardiner in Honolulu, son C.A. Park in Sydney, three grandchildren in Sydney and a granddaughter in New York City. There was no mention of her relationship with Thomas Patrick Kavanagh and her abandonment of Charlton James Park, or her own prison incarceration, no doubt the true reasons behind her assumed identity.

Regrettably I have not been able to find any images of Kavanagh or the key players in his story. Perhaps fittingly, all I can show are the gravestone images of his family in Melbourne, and of Alice Rosa Park in Honolulu.

PARK
1844—1921
PEACE

Reuben Leslie Keirl (1861-1937)

In the 1851 English census Benjamin Keirl, his wife Susan (nee Ham) and their two children (son George and baby Lydia) were living in Ben's hometown of Othery in Somerset. Benjamin worked as a "farmer's servant".

On September 13th 1851 Benjamin Keirle arrived in Victoria Australia on 'Reliance' with his wife and two children. Presumably baby Lydia died soon after, and nothing more is known of her. A mystery son (Sydney) was probably born around 1853 to 1855 in Victoria. The first identifiable recorded birth is that of Mary Emma in 1854. A second son Charles was born in 1856 but he died in 1877. Reuben was the youngest son of Benjamin and Susan, born at Ballarat East in 1861.

Benjamin worked as a labourer until his death at Sebastopol, Ballarat in 1898. Eldest son George did likewise (he died in 1923) and he inherited the £50 in real estate left by Benjamin in Albert Street Sebastopol (Susan had died in 1887). Sydney made his own way in Ballarat, working for the railways until his death in 1935. Benjamin, Susan, son Charles, daughter Frances Charlotte and son George all lie together in Buninyong Cemetery. Both George (who was at one stage a local councilor) and Sydney were well-regarded in their communities. Reuben was the restless “black sheep" of the family.

Reuben first appears in newspapers in January 1878. He was crossing a railway line at Ballarat with some cousins when he saw a man lying on the rails, shook him and got him up and out of danger. The unhappy man (who was presumably insane or attempting suicide) swore “like a bullock driver” at his rescuer. The next we hear of Reuben is in March 1881 when he passed his literary work as a pupil teacher for the third class in Ballarat.

Described in ‘Table Talk’ on March 14th 1890 as “being endowed by nature with the gift o’ the gab in an eminent degree, and of an extremely nervo-energetic type”, Reuben would not be content with a teaching career. His parents were Wesleyans, and Reuben figured as a lay preacher before being admitted on probation to the Presbyterian Church as a missionary. He was occasionally sent to fill preaching vacancies in the country for the Presbyterian Church, while during the week he officiated as a bookkeeper to a wealthy old gentleman named Martin at Malvern and then Dr. James Cox in Collins Street Melbourne.

Reuben Keirl was appointed to a church at Inglewood, where he was reportedly “fluent, energetic, and to all outward appearances very sincere in his work”. However, several serious complaints were made about his lack of truthfulness, and to prevent further inquiry he resigned his position. The ‘Lilydale Express’ of March 12th 1890 states that one of the parishioners who believed in Keirl presented him with a parcel of shares as a parting gift, and that Reuben was able to sell the shares for “more money than he had ever known in his life”.

Keirl now returned to Melbourne and posed (perhaps commencing studies) as a medical student. In September 1887 he testified at an inquest into the supposed suicide of one Laura Swain, describing himself as a medical student at Trinity College. He had supposedly washed her body after asking Dr. Neild for permission to attend the autopsy. He stated that Laura (whom he had met before on several occasions) had admitted her suicidal thoughts to him on a bridge in June 1887, but he later admitted to Detective Considine that this suicidal confession was "pure moonshine". Reuben enjoyed delivering lectures (presumably on medicine) in the Maryborough District when asked.

Keirl dropped his medical career as suddenly as he had dropped his ministry, and plunged into the mad speculation of the land boom. For a time he was associated with a partner as a land and estate agent in Collins Street East. When the partnership dissolved, he carried on in his own name at Burke & Wills Chambers in Collins Street. His first land ventures were successful, and he set up a pony stud. By good luck one of his ponies was of a record-breaking order, but his gambling fortunes reversed and he returned to his land agency work. He also became a director of an ill-fated publication known as the 'Sporting Wire'. In August 1888 and June 1889 he was reportedly intending to stand as a candidate for the parliamentary seats of East Wimmera and Grenville, but nothing came of this.

In August 1889 shareholders of the 'Preston Railway Land Company' resolved to register their company. As a land agent and promoter of the company, Reuben Keirl took over full control of its finances. In early February 1890 a newspaper reported that Keirl had written to them from Melbourne. He would soon be leaving for England to claim a £25,000 legacy for his father after the death of his uncle Charles Westlake Keirl, and he intended to then enter Edinburgh University and take his medical degree. Probably this ridiculous story was designed as an alibi if he absconded should his frauds come to light. Reuben was to use the name Westlake at various times in his life – it was his paternal grandmother's family name.

On August 30th 1889 Reuben Keirl had copied a legitimate promissory note signed by Preston Railway Land Company directors Sir Archibald Michie and Mr. Charles Chapman. On the same day he took the forged order (payable to himself) to a money lender named Mark Moss, intending it as security for a loan to pay his debts. Moss wished to check the veracity of the document with the company's solicitors. Keirl followed him to their office and told him to forget the request before he could enquire. When rumours of the transaction reached Michie he questioned Moss (who was prepared to destroy the forgery) and decided to prosecute. The company shareholders met on March 10th 1890, and Keirl broke down in tears, admitting his guilt and imploring the meeting to spare him for the sake of his relatives. Late on the night of that same day (or early the next morning) detectives arrested Reuben at the 'Palace Hotel' and took him to his house in Nicholson Street Fitzroy to search for any other incriminating paperwork.

The 'Argus' of March 12th 1890 insisted that, "the greatest sympathy is felt for his relatives who have been placed in very unpleasant positions over and over again in consequence of Keirl's vagaries". He was granted bail, and at trial in the Court of General Sessions on June 9th 1890 the "nattily-clad figure" of Reuben attempted to blame another clerk for the forgery. It was proven that the other clerk had already absconded before August 30th 1889. The defense case was that there was no direct evidence that Keirl had forged the note, and it had not actually been uttered to Moss because Keirl withdrew the request. The judge summed up adversely and he was found guilty and sentenced to four years in prison with hard labour. He was discharged from Melbourne Gaol on July 18th 1893. Showing that Keirl was not utterly bereft of goodness, earlier in July he had rushed to the assistance of an overseer at Pentridge Prison when he was attacked by five other inmates.

Reuben Keirl was very keen on the ladies, and in April 1894 he was assaulted by two brothers named Healey, who insisted that he was annoying their sister (to whom he was at one time engaged). Moving on from Miss Healey, on December 31st 1895 he married machinist Elizabeth Linda Allen in Melbourne. Linda believed that Reuben was secretary to the Medical Transfer Association of Australasia, but she soon discovered that he was merely a "turf tipster". On June 9th 1900 she sued for divorce, on the grounds that Reuben had left her continuously deserted for five years and had undergone frequent convictions for crime. He left her without support and only spent around three nights with her after their marriage (there were unsurprisingly no children). She wanted him to provide her with a home, and after she wrote to the Inspector General in March 1897 over maintenance issues, Reuben wrote to her brother Jack Allen from prison and stated that this quenched all his affection for her. In a cynical move, rather than pay maintenance to Elizabeth Linda, after his release from prison on June 14th 1900 Reuben persuaded her to reconcile with him and they would live together. He intended to do all in his power to redeem the past, and the 1900 divorce suit was dropped.

After his release from gaol in July 1893, Reuben took on the name Dr. Westlake and traveled between Melbourne and Sydney peddling his seasickness remedy. Then he set up an office in Elizabeth Street as a turf tipster named E. Gorry (a jockey who now lived in Sydney). By 1896 newspapers reported that he was "living in great style in the city" with a buggy and a fine pair of ponies. On Thursday January 23rd 1896 he attempted to deposit a cheque in the name of Gorry for £10 at the Kew branch of the National Bank. He drew several small cheques on this, which were all dishonoured. One cheque was to his regular tobacconist, who also believed that his customer was secretary to a Medical Institute at a salary of £300 per annum. He was arrested for forging and uttering at his Elizabeth Street office on January 29th, begging hard to be let off because he had only just married and he held a power of attorney from Gorry to sign cheques on his behalf. At the City Court on January 30th he pleaded guilty to obtaining goods from the tobacconist by false pretenses and was sentenced to six months with hard labour. More charges were pending.

At Kew Police Court on February 5th 1896 Keirl represented himself as a secretary to the Victorian Medical Association and a commission agent. He pleaded guilty to imposing upon the National Bank manager at Kew and received an extra three months' sentence. He still faced the forgery trial. He declared that at the conclusion of his term of imprisonment "his friends would arrange for his departure from Australia forever".

On February 11th 1896 charges of obtaining money from farmer Henry Schultz by false pretenses in August 1893 were also brought against Reuben Keirl. He had conned Schultz over shares in "Westlake's Sea Sickness Preventative" (supposedly patented). Using fake cheques, Keirl again conned Schultz in May and December 1895 and in October 1895 he obtained a music box using false pretenses. Keirl admitted to hypnotizing Schultz to get what he wanted. On February 29th 1896 he was sentenced to three years prison for false pretenses and two years extra for larceny as a bailee (obtaining the music box saying he would raffle it but pawning it for himself). These were to be added to the existing nine months' sentence. After his release on June 14th 1900 and his sudden reconciliation with his wife, one more entry is shown on Reuben's prison record. On September 27th 1901 he was sentenced to indefinite imprisonment as a Sheriff's Debtor, but he was released the following day. I cannot find any mention of this in newspapers.

On September 11th 1904 Reuben Keirl was managing a sacred concert at the 'Bijou Theatre' in Melbourne when he allowed too many people to attend for safety. He was fined. In 1912 Elizabeth Linda stated that after their reconciliation they had traveled to South Australia and Tasmania when he worked as a concert manager. Apparently friendly with the Victorian state Premier Thomas Bent (himself a keen land speculator), in late January 1906 Reuben obtained through that luminary a position as traveling advertising show agent for the Strathkellar and Wyuna closer settlement estates. Bent was to pay Keirl a government grant of £50 for six months' work giving lantern views of estates acquired by the government. The 'Closer Settlement Board' knew nothing about it and by the end of January the engagement had been cancelled. Before the appointment Keirl was said to be already "on tour for tradesmen" as a "lantern advertising agent".

On April 20th 1906 the 'Argus' reported upon yet another attempt by Elizabeth Linda Keirl to obtain maintenance from her husband at Carlton. This was the third time in the last three years. Around two to three years prior she obtained an order for £1 per week but then they again reconciled and separated. He worked as an advertising agent for 'Roche & Co' and while he stated that his salary was thirty shillings per week, his wife said that he always had plenty of money. This time he had left her without support for five weeks, and in court he implied that she was involved with another man. Reuben was not allowed to say how much he received for his closer settlement advertising, and he had recently given an entertainment at Government House. The Bench ordered him to pay his wife ten shillings per week.

In March 1907 newspapers were complaining that Reuben Keirl and another entertainer were allowed by the Minister of Education to use State Schools for purposes of gramophone entertainments. The Minister denied having anything to do with it. Reuben was hoping to accompany Premier Bent as a lanternist with a biograph and magic lantern on his impending lecture tour of Great Britain. Bent denied such an intention. Shortly before his departure, Bent purchased three gramophones from Keirl for £45 (without the usual tender process) purportedly for the use of the insane in Victorian asylums. Reuben was to lend some of his own cylinders to the asylums but the medical superintendents declined to take responsibility for their care and the gramophones remained silent until late April when the Acting Treasurer approved purchase of some records. By the end of March 1907, Keirl was saying that his impending departure for England had nothing to do with the Premier's tour. He now abandoned his voyage to avoid any embarrassment to Bent.

In September 1907 Keirl applied for permission to run a motorboat on the lake at Albert Park in South Melbourne, for passenger traffic. On December 28th he exhibited a picture show at the 'Gaiety Theatre'. In January 1909 he dashed up to Pentridge in Premier Bent's car to announce certain privileges for warders (an election loomed). In February he was promoter of a boxing match in Ballarat. In June (Bent lost office) his permission to give Melba song recitals and lectures in State Schools was withdrawn. Bent died in September 1909, and in December 1909 Reuben Keirl and three other plaintiffs sued Madame Melba for refusing to sing at an Exhibition as had been arranged while Bent was still in office. In June 1911, Reuben Keirl was again issuing post-dated cheques, which were dishonoured.

In March 1912 he again deserted his long-suffering wife Elizabeth Linda (she last saw him on March 6th when he said he was going away on business) and for this he was arrested on April 12th. They had been living at Holmes Street in Brunswick, and were moving after Reuben sold the house. Reuben had allegedly mortgaged all her furniture to pay his debts, and she had given him more money from the bank for the debts as well.

At Carlton Court on April 17th 1912 Lizzy stated that she was left without financial support, that her husband earned very good money on commission as a collector for the 'Ragged Boys' Home', and that he was "selling houses at the beginning of last year". She had been earning £1 per week at canvassing, but was now "too worried" to work. Reuben accused her of improper relations with Mr. James ("an old game of his" said his wife) while Lizzy accused him of living with Miss Alice Olive Tregardh in the country (they had stayed together beforehand at the 'Salvation Army Metropole' hotel as a married couple) and giving her jewellery. Lizzy had recommenced divorce proceedings. Keirl had been beaten by Mr. James (who was employed by Lizzy's brothers to trace Reuben and serve the divorce papers) and by Alice's brother. He lost his collecting job for the Boys' Home after Lizzy took proceedings against him. Reuben would counter-sue for divorce and cite three co-respondents (prompting laughter in the court). He was ordered to pay fifteen shillings per week maintenance until the divorce came through. On May 24th 1912 the divorce hearing on the grounds of misconduct took place. Elizabeth (a machinist and artist) was now living in Drummond Street Carlton. Reuben was unemployed and no order was made for alimony.

At Ballarat on December 2nd 1912 Keirl (a "land salesman living in Melbourne") sued the superintendent of the Benevolent Asylum for money payable after the sale of a gramophone and records (he won but was ordered to pay court costs). In Melbourne on Wednesday December 4th, Reuben Keirl (now living in Mitchell Street Brunswick) lodged a complaint with detectives. Alice Olive Tregardh had thrown vitriol over him, burning his clothes and body. He was walking in Albion Street with his ex-wife when he met Olly (living with her parents in Holmes Street Brunswick), who asked to talk to him. He refused and she followed him. Olive, well known in local church circles, now accused Reuben of using insulting words and threatening to take her life (prior to the vitriol affair). On June 19th in a grocer's shop in Albion Street Brunswick he had said to her "if ever you betray me I will see you in your coffin".

At Brunswick Police Court on December 18th 1912 the ex-lovers (who last spoke on April 12th due to objections and threats by her parents, despite his request for forgiveness from them) appeared. Through his solictor, Keirl had requested on November 29th 1912 the return of jewellery and money worth £25 from Olly. Tregardh met Keirl (posing as George Gould) two years earlier when he offered to drive her to Sunday School as he lived in the same street as her family. Instead he drove her out to Sunbury, introduced her to a man as his wife and threatened to tell her father that she allowed this if she did not comply with his wishes. Keirl denied this and said that Olive had asked him to take her away from her family, where she was kept as "a white slave". She supposedly developed an infatuation with the older man, now a "land salesman". He was not living with his divorced wife but saw her frequently and considered her "a wronged woman". Keirl was fined for the insulting words and the threatening language charge was dismissed.

On December 19th 1912 the trial of Alice Olive Tregardh continued. She said that Keirl was "always waylaying and threatening her", that she had bought the vitriol to frighten him, and that on December 4th it was he who had called her aside, saying he had something important to tell her. The only physical injury to Keirl was a burn on the back. He was always sending her letters, fruit and chocolates and waylaid her at every opportunity. He in turn produced letters from Tregardh to show that she had threatened that if he went back to "Old Liz" she would have his life's blood. The bench consulted and the chairman discharged the accused. The large crowd inside and outside the court cheered, and Olly's mother fainted. Immediately there were talks of an appeal, because the bench had given no reasons or explanations for the decision, which was based on partisanship rather than evidence. On February 13th 1913 the Crown filed a presentment against Miss Tregardh, who would stand trial at the next sitting of the Supreme Court. On March 4th 1913 a jury returned a verdict of "not guilty" against her on the charge of intent to do grievous bodily harm. Keirl insisted that during the time they had lived together "there were no immoral relations" between them and hence he had not "ruined her". Faced with his criminal past, Reuben stated that Sir Thomas Bent had befriended him because he knew that he was falsely convicted of forgery in 1890. Prior to leaving the dock, Alice Olive declared that letters purportedly signed by her and produced in the previous trial were forgeries. In summing up, the Chief Justice had no praise for either the victim or the accused.

In June 1913 Reuben Keirl (estate agent) was again in trouble over dishonoured cheques. In July he was ordered to pay a woman monies owing on historical land transactions. He was a land agent and manager of a picture company. On August 12th 1913 he was a "traveler for picture shows" when he was punched by a man named Thomas Ireland in the street in Brunswick. Ireland said he was protecting Miss Tregardh from Keirl's continued unwanted attentions and offensive statements. The assault charge against Ireland was dismissed (without comment by the bench). Keirl was still visiting his divorced wife, who was now calling herself Linda Allen. This seems to have marked the end of relations between Olly Tregardh and Reuben Keirl. She married in Victoria in 1925 and died in 1952.

Later in August 1913 Reuben was again before the court over outstanding debts from an old dishonoured cheque court order. In late August he was still holding possibly dodgy picture entertainments for charity. In October 1913 Kyneton police wished to proceed against Reuben Keirl, who had no lawful visible means of support, over his charity fundraisers. He reportedly sent a postcard from Auckland indicating that he had left for America, but I feel sure that he never left Australian shores.

An “R. Kierl" caught the boat 'Warilla' from Melbourne to Sydney, arriving on September 18th 1913. Later newspapers tell us that Reuben Keirl was in Albury New South Wales in May 1914, when he took moving pictures of the flight of Frenchman Guillaux over the town on May 23rd. 'Truth' on October 30th 1915 published a document showing that on September 16th 1914 Reuben Keirl had become attached to the Australian Army Medical Corps in their camp at Queen’s Park in Waverley, Sydney. For one seeking glory, the war provided perfect opportunities, but Reuben was too old for active service. He was appointed as canteen officer to Troopship A41 under Captain John Buchanan, and in this capacity left Melbourne on December 21st 1914 for Albany Western Australia. He was arrested at Albany on New Year’s Eve 1914 for unlawfully wearing a military uniform. On January 12th 1915 in Albany he was fined £10, in default of which he would be imprisoned. Later newspapers note that he served six weeks in prison at this time.

Keirl stated that after leaving Albany, he travelled to Brisbane on 'RMS Orontes'. The ship manifest for March 17th at Fremantle indicates that he was booked to disembark at Adelaide. In late May 1915 'Captain Kyrle' (late canteen officer of Troopship A41) was preaching and giving lectures about his "war experiences" at Brisbane and Warwick in Queensland, raising money for "the Belgian fund". He seems to have visited Adelaide in South Australia and Goulburn in New South Wales on a similar mission in April and early May 1915. On April 14th he delivered a lecture (with his Emden photos) at the 'Victoria Hall' in Adelaide for the 'Children's Hospital Board' (to which he gave a gramophone and some records) thanks to the patronage of Chief Justice Sir. Samuel Way after an interview at 'Montefiore'. His lectures for two Methodist churches in Adelaide in April 1915 were also advertised. He collected funds for the 'Central Methodist Mission' in Adelaide but did not seem to take any of the proceeds for himself.

On August 26th 1915 the good Captain (a "dapper little man") delivered an address at the 'Caulfield Grammar School' in Melbourne. On Sunday September 5th 1915 this "Hero of the Dardanelles" was again talking about his war experiences at a church in St. Kilda, Melbourne. He would hold a fund raising lecture on the "Smashing of the Emden" (with lantern slides) the next night. A suspicious churchman went to visit the 'Criminal Investigation Department' and recognized Keirl from his photo. The lecture was hurriedly cancelled, and 'Captain Kyrle' headed off to Tasmania.

On September 13th 1915 Reuben Keirl (commission agent) was sentenced to 48 hours imprisonment for false pretences at Devonport. He had visited state schools in Launceston and on the North West coast of Tasmania, giving talks and inviting head teachers to sell picture postcards of warships (promising that the schools would be presented with enlarged versions). He was ordered to leave the state, and departed for Melbourne on 'Oonah' on September 15th 1915.

As soon as he arrived in Victoria, Keirl continued his unauthorized visits to state schools, selling postcards of the 'Emden' to "collect funds for charitable purposes". On September 21st 1916 he appeared before Melbourne's City Court, charged with wearing clothing intended to resemble a naval uniform. He had been walking about in Melbourne in the "uniform" for three weeks. He declared that he had been on three troopships (as canteen officer, patrol officer and captain's steward), had been four times through the Mediterranean, and was due to re-join his current troopship in New Zealand. He had been discharged from that ship at Port Fairy with a broken leg. Carrying a fiddleback blackwood walking stick inscribed with the name of Sir Thomas Bent, he was detained in the City Watch House, then allowed bail.

At the Melbourne City Court on October 10th 1916 Reuben Keirl was fined £10 for breaching the 'War Precautions Act'. The Melbourne uniform was described as “all tinsel and gold decoration” and Keirl looked like “some high dignity of the sea (there was laughter in the court). Frederick William Allen testified that he had been fourth engineer on a transport upon which Keirl was employed as a captain’s steward. Reuben had gone ashore at Naples and at Port Said in a blue uniform and at the latter port he had delivered a lecture on Rome and the Catacombs (great laughter this time).

Reuben Keirl now adopted the alias of Charles Kyle. In this guise he gave a war lecture on his supposed troopship adventures at the Bowral Presbyterian Church in New South Wales in March 1917. On May 4th 1918, he appeared at Westminster Court in London, having been arrested by a Melbourne detective attached to Australian Headquarters in London. The detective had known him in Australia and recognized him at ‘Victoria Station’. Still using the alias Charles Kyle, Reuben had been posing in uniform as an officer of ‘HMAS Sydney’ and as an officer of the ‘Overseas Transport Service’ (when he was only a steward). In England he had been lecturing in churches (including Rev. Spurgeon’s Tabernacle) and selling pictures of the ‘Emden’. In court (in his bogus uniform) on May 8th 1918 he admitted buying the photo in the Cocos Islands, and pleaded guilty to fraudulently wearing uniforms. He testified that he had landed in London with only five shillings, and sold the souvenir photos to earn a living. He had visited schools at Caterham and sold some photos to children from St. John’s Schools, stating that he was raising money for the purchase of gramophones for troopships. He was sentenced to three months prison with hard labour.

Australian newspapers reporting upon the matter stated that Keirl was “described by one who knew him as a short, thin, spare-built man, with a persuasive manner". "He was recognised as the acme of fashion in the matter of dressing.”

On October 19th 1918 ‘Truth’ reported that Reuben Keirl was back in Melbourne again. As ‘Kyle’, the previous Sunday he had upset some nuns at a Melbourne convent by telling a war story of “questionable taste”. They then declined his offer to lecture to some Catholic schoolboys about German submarines.

On September 24th 1919 the ‘New South Wales Police Gazette’ published a photo of Reuben Keirl alias Captain Kyle, who was now in Sydney. He was recently prominently identified with the establishment in Sydney of a branch of the ‘Mercantile Marine Service Association of Australia’, which aimed to raise funds to show appreciation for merchant seamen who risked their lives in submarine zones during the war. When his past was discovered, Keirl was debarred from holding any official position with the Association, but it was feared he would use recommendations from prominent naval and military officials to visit country districts and other states to collect money. He was described as 5’6” tall and a “cook” by trade. Somehow, as Charles Westlake Kyle born in Ballarat in 1872, Reuben Keirl managed to obtain a Mercantile Marine Medal and a British Medal for his war work as a merchant seaman.

Ruben Keirl returned to Melbourne using the name Charles Westlake Kyle, and settled at 249 Mitchell Street Brunswick. In July 1920 he was threatening to sue the council over poorer street lighting when he fell. In November 1922 he gifted an autograph of Lord Kitchener (bought through public subscription, after he had earlier sold it) to the new 'Kitchener Memorial Hospital'. When Kyle was recognised as Reuben Keirl, he stated that back in 1916 he had sent Kitchener a book of hymns and received a letter of thanks with the signature, and the signature was deemed to be genuine. In 1924 Electoral rolls he is listed as Reuben Kyrle, 249 Mitchell Street Brunswick, picture proprietor. In 1931 he was at 135 Mitchell Street Coburg, and worked as a traveler. In 1935, 1936 and 1937 he lived at 20 Springhall Parade Coburg and was still a traveler. He died as Reuben Keirl, apparently unnoticed and with no estate, in August 1937.

After Reuben Keirl left Victoria in late 1913, he probably had no further contact with his ex-wife (now Miss Linda Allen). We know that she described herself as a machinist and artist during the 1912 divorce, and that she had moved to Carlton. From 1914 until 1916 Linda Allen (artist) was living at 407 Lygon Street Carlton and letting out rooms to boarders for an income. On August 5th 1916 she advertised a sale by auction of all her household furniture, kitchen utensils and even the sewing machine, because she was "relinquishing housekeeping". I believe that she moved to Petersham in Sydney and set herself up in the city as a maker of "figure appliances" (sewing garments for abdominal weakness). Calling herself

"Madame Bazain" and Elizabeth Linda Bazain, she died in Sydney as "Elizabeth Keirl, known as Linda Bazain" widow on January 2nd 1968. This woman was exactly the correct age (94) to be Elizabeth Linda Keirl (nee Allen).

January 1891

June 1893

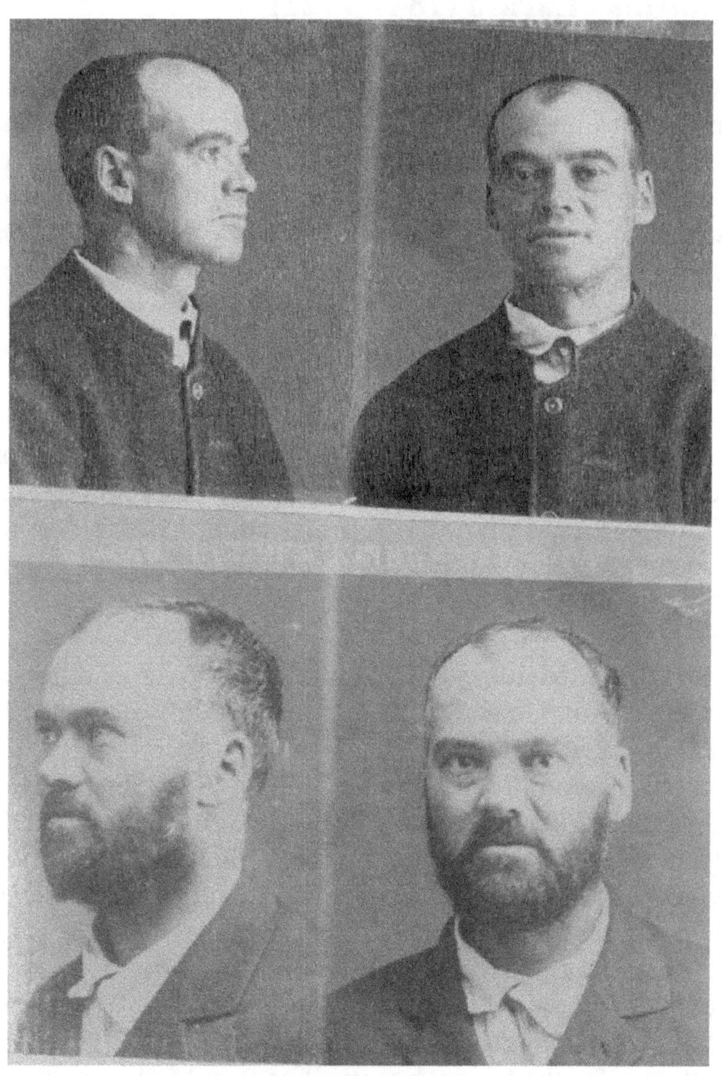

March 1896

Matthias Larkin (1847-1921)

Matthias/Matthew was born in Killaloe County Clare Ireland around 1847. His parents Michael Larkin and Anne Nash had married there on February 22nd 1846. Daughter Mary was born around 1849 and son Michael was baptized at Killaloe on November 15th 1850. On December 16th 1851 the family arrived in Victoria Australia on 'Stebonheath'. Daughter Anne was born in Victoria in 1852 and died in 1872. I am unable to find any further trace of son Michael after arrival.

In his 1966 book 'The Land Boomers' Michael Cannon states that the Larkin parents were part of the gold rush to Victoria. Finding no luck at prospecting, Michael Larkin became a dairy farmer at Emerald Hill (later South Melbourne) and did well for himself.

Eldest son Matthias was apprenticed to a saddler at Emerald Hill. He was quite a religious fellow and in 1870 he was treasurer and then honorary secretary of the church committee for the 'Irish-Australian (later Hibernian-Australasian) Catholic Benefit Society' of 'SS Peter and Paul (Masonic) Lodge'. He became involved with bowling, cricket and rowing clubs wherever he lived. In 1874 Matthias Larkin married Bridget Frances Cormick, another Irish immigrant who had arrived with her parents and siblings on 'Maryborough' in December 1863. Her father James Cormick worked as a toll-collector for the borough council of Port Melbourne from his arrival in Melbourne.

There were a spate of deaths in the Cormick family between 1886 and 1889. Bridget's younger brother John died on June 6th 1886 from inflammation of the lungs, her younger brother James died on June 19th 1886 (John's condition was probably contagious), her mother Mary (nee Delaney) died in September 1887, her older brother Michael died in March 1889 and her father James died in October 1889. Bridget probably worked as a domestic servant prior to her marriage in 1874.

On November 4th 1874 Michael Cormick Larkin was born at 176 Ferras Street Emerald Hill. Bridget clearly thought highly of her birth family and all of Matthias's children were given the middle name of Cormick/Cormack. Throughout 1875 and 1876 Matthias continued living at Ferras Street, working as a saddler while Bridget worked as a dressmaker.

From June 1875 Matthias was a committee member of the 'South Melbourne Permanent Building and Investment Society and Deposit Institute' as it issued a prospectus and began selling shares. According to Cannon (1966 above) the aim of the founders was to erect cottages for artisans in the rapidly growing area. In July 1877 Larkin became acting Secretary and from September 1877 he took on the paid position permanently.

Immediately Matthias Larkin gave up his work as a saddler and moved his family to live above the Building Society office at 170 Clarendon Street Emerald Hill. Daughter Annie Cormick Larkin was born in 1877, son

James Cormick Larkin in 1879 and son Matthew Cormick Larkin in 1880 (died August 1881). Cannon (1966) states that Larkin was tempted to make more money through the land boom, and he set up a real estate company with his private accountant Patrick Cleary at 200 Clarendon Street Emerald Hill. Cleary was a much younger man than Larkin, and they shared the same Irish great-grandparents through the Nash line. Larkin moved both his family and the office of the Building Society to that address from February 27th 1882. As well as retaining his paid position as Secretary to the Building Society he was now an auctioneer and insurance, estate and finance agent. Cleary and Larkin operated both businesses almost as one entity, for their own financial gain.

Matthias Larkin was powering ahead, and in 1881 he became the youngest magistrate in Victoria. Before his imprisonment in 1892 he proudly proclaimed that as a magistrate he had "always put men away in a scientific and gentlemanly manner". In 1886 he was elected to the 'South Melbourne City Council', a position he retained until his resignation after his arrest in November 1891. In March 1887 he moved his family residence to a mansion 'Lakeview' on Canterbury Road at Albert Park, leaving his offices at 200 Clarendon Street. At his 1892 insolvency hearing Matthias's father Michael Larkin testified that in 1887 he had lent his son £300 towards the purchase of the house but it had not been repaid. In September 1888 Joseph Cormick Larkin was born at 'Lakeview'.

At the time of his arrest in 1891 the salary of Larkin as Secretary to the Building Society was reported as £500 per annum with an allowance of about £100 for house rent and similar expenses. Problems with the Building Society only surfaced in October 1891 when Larkin was unable to present the balance sheet and statement of accounts for the financial year at the annual general meeting on October 14th, citing ill health. On Tuesday November 10th 1891 auditors approached the Building Society President Joseph Stead, who then visited Larkin at 'Lakeview' that afternoon. Larkin admitted to Stead that there were problems but that he thought he would be able to "tide it over". He would "give himself up" the following morning, as he had "done harm enough". He would not tell Stead the amount involved but it was thought to be a little over £10,000.

At 'South Melbourne Police Court' on Wednesday November 11th 1891 Matthias Larkin J.P. was charged with having falsified the Society books and thus defrauding shareholders. The father of the accused and Patrick Cleary each paid half of the £2,000 bail. Larkin had confessed to his falsifications and thought the amount might be over £10,000. There was shock at the felony committed by "one of the most popular citizens" of the city renowned as "kindly, genial and perfectly honest".

On December 10th 1891 a meeting of shareholders and depositors heard that auditors had already discovered defalcations of £54,904. Joseph Stead was now an invalid. The 'Argus' of December 11th explained that since 1887 balance sheets had been falsified and Larkin had “systematically and unceasingly” appropriated funds for his own use through “complicated and clever devices”. Suspecting that his private accountant Patrick Cleary must have been aware of his irregular proceedings, authorities arrested him on December 11th for conspiring to defraud the Building Society. Larkin was re-arrested on additional charges, and this time bail was too high to be met.

The 'Herald' of December 16th 1891 reveals the difference in character between the two accused as they appeared in the courtroom. Larkin was “dressed in a light summer suit, and appeared to feel his position very lightly". Cleary “on the other hand, betrayed more feeling and anxiety”. The 'Herald’ of February 29th 1892 again commented on the two accused in court. Larkin was "a jolly-looking, stout, well-conditioned man, dressed in a fashionable Beaufort suit, new as a new pin, a dainty scarf was daintily tied under his spotless linen collar, and the snowy cuffs came down to the wrists. He looked as happy as Larry, and no sign of uneasiness was apparent on his countenance”. Cleary “on the other hand, was much more plainly dressed. His beard had lost its careful trim, and he looked restlessly around the court”.

On December 18th 1891 Matthias Larkin was declared insolvent due to losses in the purchase of real estate that had depreciated in value and the consequent inability to realize the pressure of creditors. His liabilities were estimated at £18,000 and his assets at £13,000. In January 1892 his debts were proven to be £46,031. His suspect land transactions were uncovered by the 'South Melbourne Citizen' in February 1892, and were subsequently examined by the 'Insolvency Court' as attempts to hide assets. On November 12th 1891 Matthias had transferred two cottages in Young Street worth £1,214 to fellow Building Society director George Gray, to pay a debt. Patrick Cleary's estate was sequestered in April 1892 and he too was insolvent. By May 1893 the liquidators of the "South Melbourne Building and Investment Society" believed that Larkin and Cleary were responsible for the disappearance of over £100,000 of the society's money. Liquidation of the Society finally ended in the 'Practice Court' on November 2nd 1905.

On March 2nd 1892 the first trial of Larkin and Cleary ended when the jury disagreed. The charge was that between March 4th 1888 and August 16th 1889 they had conspired to defraud the Building Society of £2,322 1s 11d. There were twenty-one specific acts involved. Both accused pleaded not guilty. The money was used to erect buildings on land at Howe Crescent. On March 4th 1892 four bondsmen (including Michael Larkin and Matthias himself) succeeded in obtaining Matthias's release on £4,000 bail. The accused "went away with his friends, looking not only unconcerned but radiant". Cleary remained in 'Melbourne Gaol'.

A guilty verdict resulted at the second trial on Wednesday March 23rd 1892. The next day Cleary was sentenced to four years' prison and Larkin to six years. On August 23rd 1894 Larkin was sentenced to an additional five years imprisonment on extra charges of stealing a Building Society cheque for £3,398 10s 8d on May 16th 1889. Cleary was released on March 14th 1895, and he immediately took his wife and children to Sydney to make a new start as a newsagent at Woollahra. Prior to his 1891 arrest he had been proprietor of the 'Kyneton Observer', the auditor for several important institutions, a well-known literary man and one of the best authorities on Australasian history. In Sydney he admirably put his past behind him, became a "doyen of catholic journalism" and was awarded two Papal honours.

By November 1899 Matthias Larkin was due for release from Pentridge but on May 9th 1892 he had been found guilty of contempt when he refused to answer questions in the 'Insolvency Court'. He now agreed to answer all questions on his trade dealings and estate and was released on bail on December 5th 1899, to be examined by the 'Insolvency Court' on February 5th 1900. During his time in prison, his mother Anne Larkin (nee Nash) had died in April 1894.

Matthias Larkin's estate had been voluntarily sequestered on December 17th 1891. 'Lakeview' had been put up for auction in January 1892, complete with furniture, a grand piano, billiard table and statues. In May 1892 Michael Larkin had been examined by the 'Insolvency Court' to see if he had helped to hide assets of his son. He had initially taken the piano and a safe from 'Lakeview' but these had since been removed from his house, and he had sold Matthias's library in his own name for £153 (which went to the solicitor). In September 1893 it was Bridget Frances Larkin's turn. She was then living in a house in

Park Street South Melbourne taken for her by Michael Larkin. She kept a boarding house and eldest son Michael Cormick Larkin (still a student) earned a little money sometimes. When she could not pay the rent Michael Larkin paid it for her. She had a little property of her own before her marriage but had acquired no property since.

In February 1900 Matthias Larkin submitted a schedule stating that his assets totaled £34,462 and his debts were £27,161 leaving a surplus of £7,300. With no more mention of Matthias we must presume that he was now allowed to resume a normal life. In his absence Bridget had worked as a draper, and she and the younger children were living with Michael Cormick Larkin at 233 Malvern Road South Yarra in 1896 when he was admitted to practice as a solicitor and barrister (he represented his father in court after that). Michael set up his practice at "Stalbridge Chambers" 443 Chancery Lane in October 1897, and by 1905 he had acquired a partner named Reynolds.

The Larkins family stuck together, even after the release of Matthias. In 1903 they all lived at 233 Malvern Road and Matthias had established himself as an estate agent at 424 Chapel Street South Yarra. Bridget still worked as a draper. By 1909 they had all moved to Balwyn, where Bridget and Annie kept house. James worked as a surveyor, Matthias as an accountant, Joseph as a clerk and Michael as a barrister.

By 1910 the family was living at 'Norwood' Cotham Road Kew, where Joseph was a clerk, Matthias a law clerk working for 'Reynolds & Larkin' and Michael a solicitor. Michael Larkin (father of Matthias) died on August 3rd 1910. He was still living in Park Street South Melbourne and 'Reynolds & Larkin' administered the estate of £404 net. This went to Matthias's unmarried sister Mary, a music teacher, who died in 1931. In 1911 James Cormick Larkin married his cousin Margaret Agatha Cormick (the daughter of Bridget's brother John). James worked as a surveyor and civil engineer until his death at Fitzroy in 1961.

By 1919 the family had moved to 116 Victoria Road Auburn. Matthias still worked as a law clerk, Bridget and Annie did not work, Joseph was an accountant and Michael was a barrister. Matthias died on November 1st 1921. Bridget died on May 22nd 1926. Joseph Cormick Larkin married in 1924 and died at Ballarat in 1962. He had been a well-known footballer in Victoria. Michael and Annie never married, and continued to live together until Michael's death in April 1941. Annie died in 1958.
In a family plot at 'Melbourne General Cemetery' lie Michael Larkin senior (died 1910) and his wife Anne (nee Nash, died 1894) in one grave and in the other lie their daughter Annie who died in 1872, Matthias, Bridget (nee Cormick) and Mary who died in 1931.

The Larkin plot MGC

Matthias Larkin 1892

Patrick Cleary 1892

James Mann (1901-1947)

James Mann was born at Broken Hill in New South Wales on June 29th 1901, the second son of James and Ellen (nee Doyle). By 1902 the family had moved to Western Australia, where James senior tried mining in Kalgoorlie and then worked as a labourer for Perth tramways until his death in March 1923 (he was survived by his widow Ellen and nine children).

The 'Mirror' (Perth) of June 24th 1933 stated that James Mann junior had been educated at one of Perth's leading schools, where he shone both in his studies and in athletics. After leaving school he reportedly entered the office of a leading financier, who states that Mann was "one of the smartest, best behaved and most attentive lads ever in my employ" before his early fall from grace. All of this sounds rather unlikely. By the age of sixteen he was working as a shop assistant for a Perth pawnbroker. In November 1916 he was arrested at York on a train from Perth for the theft of £35. The 'Mirror' (Perth) of November 4th 1939 states that the pawnbroker's assistant was very intelligent and popular with customers, and on two separate occasions he was given a chance after taking property from his employer. He had appeared in the Perth 'Children's Court' on several occasions and eventually was given the chance to go east after a vagrancy charge.

The New South Wales gaol record for James Mann (under the alias of Michael Foy) notes that in 1916 (by his own account) he had been sentenced in Brisbane

Queensland to two months with hard labour for vagrancy, but was released as a first offender. I cannot verify this, but if so it was probably in Perth. The NSW record also shows that Mann (using an unverifiable alias) was convicted of stealing at Central Police Court in Sydney on December 12th 1917 and paid the fine of £3 immediately.

In January 1918 in Sydney, as Michael Foy he was arrested for breaking and entering a dwelling house with intent to steal. At the Sydney Quarter Sessions on January 28th 1918 he pleaded guilty and asked for leniency on account of his youth. He was sentenced to twelve months with hard labour at Goulburn Gaol, but was clearly released earlier. In early December 1918 he was before another court in Carlton in Melbourne for larceny. His Victorian prison record is under the name of James Mann. At Carlton Police Court on December 6th 1918 he was sentenced to two months imprisonment on four counts of larceny and attempted larceny. From Melbourne Gaol, on December 19th 1918 he was taken to trial at Yea in Victoria for having picked a pocket at the Yea Show on November 21st. He was sentenced to twelve months prison for larceny from the person.

On June 25th 1921 James Mann (alias Lewis) was working as a salesman in Brisbane when he was arrested for the theft of a roll of blue serge cloth earlier that month. Some time during 1921 he married young Brisbane widow Edith (Edie/Elsie) Martha Northover (nee Mason) at Redfern in Sydney under his correct name. Edith was born in 1898 but during her time with

Mann she reduced her age by a couple of years. Her husband, Brisbane jockey Frederick Northover, had died in France during the war in September 1917 and in September 1919 she published a tribute of love to his memory in a Brisbane newspaper. At Brisbane Supreme Court on August 2nd 1921 the "well dressed young man" (Mann alias Lewis) was sentenced to twelve months in prison.

After his release from prison, Mann turned from outright thieving to card-sharping. On October 2nd 1922 he was charged at Port Melbourne Court with frequenting a public place with intent to commit a felony. On Saturday September 30th he had been a passenger on the steamer 'Esperance Bay' traveling from Sydney to Melbourne when he and another man cheated at poker. Detectives testified that both the accused were "well known interstate magsmen, and were reputed cheats and pickpockets". Because the accuser had sailed for England and could not testify in court, on October 9th 1922 Mann and his co-accused were instead charged with being idle and disorderly, and having no lawful means of support. Mann protested that he had recently left a position as fruit salesman in Adelaide. He had savings of £130 of which his wife retained £100. The Bench was not satisfied, both accused admitted prior convictions, and they were sentenced to six months in prison.

In August 1923 at Seymour Police Court in Victoria James Mann was fined for playing an unlawful card game for money on a train between Seymour and Melbourne. On January 9th 1924 he was at it again on the

'Melbourne Express' from Sydney, using the alias John Doyle. At 'Goulburn Court' on January 21st, Detective Robinson testified that Mann/Doyle was of 'bad character" and had been frequenting Sydney's Central Railway Station. Mann's wife sat in the public gallery. Giving his own testimony, Mann said that he had been married for three years and lived in Brisbane where he worked as a salesman. He produced a roll of notes totaling £208 and a hawker's license valid for Queensland and Victoria. He had a half-interest in a hairdressing business in Sydney with Harold George Cowley, and won money gambling on racehorses. Edie Mann produced a bank passbook showing credit of £490 in her name. Her husband had recently won £400 on the races in Melbourne. With nothing to show that Mann was idle and disorderly, the charges were dismissed.

On Saturday June 28th 1924 twenty men were arrested at a gaming house in Melbourne, among them a clerk aged twenty two named James Mann. On the premises were portable phones, betting tickets and gambling apparatus. Presumably Mann was fined.

On Tuesday August 12th 1924 James Mann used obscene language to Detective Grieve at Spencer Street Station, when card playing on trains was discussed. He was arrested and fined £10 the next day. Grieve stated that the "bouncing, impudent young man" was in company with well-known thieves and had been convicted a fortnight earlier for working the trains.

On July 21st 1947 the 'Herald' (Melbourne) stated that James Mann was sentenced to six months on two counts of stealing in 1927, after which he cleared out from Melbourne and went to England. Several British newspapers of the same date picked up the same information, but I am unable to find anything relevant to Mann or his known aliases between August 1924 and July 17th 1929. On that date the 'New South Wales Police Gazette' published a photo of James Mann alias Michael Foy who was wanted by customs at Sydney for obtaining false passports. He was described as a "bogus land salesman and confidence man". Later newspaper articles stated that when Mann went to Britain he studied at etiquette school and cultivated an "Oxford accent" to fit him for his role as a continental confidence trickster. He may have done this prior to his return to Australia in 1929.

On January 1st 1929 Edith Martha Northover arrived in Fremantle from Port Said in Egypt on 'Cathay'. Her home address was Darvall Street in Brisbane. No doubt she used her old name because her husband was wanted by authorities. He may or may not have returned on the same ship (under an alias). Customs must not have tried very hard to find James Mann, as he returned to Brisbane undisturbed and by November 1932 was regarded as Brisbane's "most dashing better". (In September 1932 he was described in a newspaper as "a visitor from America" when he donated a handsome cup for the winner of a horse race at 'Hedley Park' in Brisbane.)

On November 6th 1932 the 'Sunday Mail' (Brisbane) stated that the Charleville racehorse 'Polly Speck' had made his first appearance in Brisbane. James Mann was so impressed with the galloper that he secured a lease on the horse on high terms. On November 24th 1932 the 'Daily Telegraph' (Sydney) noted that 'Polly Speck' was entered for important summer handicap races at Randwick in Sydney. Jimmy Mann was much discussed in northern racing circles as he had recently given Brisbane bookmakers such a drubbing that he now had a huge following.

By 1932 Edith Mann was traveling internationally with Jimmy's youngest sister Veronica Margaret Mann (born in Perth in August 1918). James and Edith had no children and Veronica probably provided company for his wife while he independently perpetrated his confidence tricks. Veronica also apparently enjoyed their high-living lifestyle. On January 12th 1932 Edith Northover and Veronica Mann arrived in Fremantle from Marseilles on 'Narkunda'. Edith gave her home address at St Kilda in Melbourne and Veronica gave her mother's address in Perth.

On May 17th 1932 James Mann alias Coates allegedly perpetrated a swindle in France on a man named Watson. Accounts of the swindle vary – initially the victim was an Australian sheep farmer named James Watson. Later it was an English baronet named Sir Michael Watson. The 'Herald' (Melbourne) of July 21st 1947 said that Mann boasted about conning Watson (who lived in the south of France) of 3¾ million francs, beginning on a cruise from

Alexandria to Marseilles and finishing at Watson's banker's in Paris two days later. Some sources say that the swindle related to currency speculation, others to a scheme to revolutionize the docking of ships.

Mann/Coates and his accomplice were booked to return to Australia from London on 'Cormorin' in July 1932, but detectives found only Edith Martha Northover and Veronica Mann on the ship, which arrived in Fremantle on July 19th 1932. Both gave their destination on the ship's manifest as Veronica and Jim's mother's address in Perth. The 'Mirror' (Perth) of June 24th 1933 states that detectives followed Edith and Veronica to Brisbane, where Edith deposited a large sum into a bank account. It was assumed that James Mann crossed to America from England before rejoining his wife in Brisbane.

'Truth' (Brisbane) on August 24th 1952 stated that the horse 'Polly Speck' was one of the few costly mistakes of Jimmy Mann's life. This was because he was arrested at 'Victoria Park' racecourse in Sydney on May 24th 1933 when he took the horse down to race there. The arrest was on the 1932 Paris swindle charge, and Mann (alias Foy, Mason or Coates) was remanded in 'Long Bay Gaol' awaiting extradition to France. He was released on July 7th 1933 after French authorities dropped proceedings.

Oddly, Mann was described as a "motor mechanic" in newspapers in 1933. He may have already begun to establish his firm 'Coates Autos and Finance Co" in Melbourne by then. The company was advertising by

October 1934 and the family (including Veronica) was living in a luxury Toorak mansion. James Coates now described himself as a "financier", raced horses in Melbourne and traveled overseas alone while Edith and Veronica traveled separately (Edith now using the surname Coates).

In late December 1936, Edith and Veronica traveled from Australia on 'Aorangi' to America and were to meet James Coates at his usual residence the 'Ambassador Hotel' in Los Angeles (he had come earlier in the month on 'Europa' from Germany). Similarly, James Coates traveled to Los Angeles in December 1937 on 'Monterey' and Edith and Veronica were to join him at the 'Amassador Hotel' when they arrived on 'Mariposa' in January 1938. They all gave contact details on ship manifests designed to mislead any authorities looking for James. Society articles in Australian newspapers in March 1937 mentioned that Mrs. Coates of Toorak and her sister Veronica Mann ("two attractive Melbourne residents") had returned to Sydney from Hollywood after a nine-month tour of America. Miss Mann was studying singing and the pair had met many famous film stars.

In November 1936 Mann/Coates alias Agnew was alleged to have swindled an Austrian nobleman (now a British national) named Prince Jean Sapieha out of £12,000 in Switzerland. In Basel he had posed as an Australian financier and adviser and the swindle involved racehorses. Identified by a photograph, in March 1939 as James Mann (a mechanic of Gloucester Place London) he appeared at Bow Street Station in London on a provisional extradition warrant from Switzerland. Affidavits from Australia swore that at the time of the supposed crime Mann was in Australia (and at the Melbourne Cup on November 3rd 1936). We know that as James Coates he left Bremen in Germany on 'Europa' on November 27th 1936. When the Swiss authorities did not bother to send a representative in a case "bristling with difficulties" Mann was discharged from the Bow Street Court. Presumably at the request of Prince Sapieha, and despite Mann's release from Bow Street in March 1939, Scotland Yard later issued a request for his re-arrest.

The 'Herald' (Melbourne) of July 21st 1947 stated that Coates/Mann was finally warned off Melbourne racecourses because of his criminal associates, and that shortly before war broke out in 1939 he sold his Toorak mansion and his finance business and went abroad. On September 29th 1939 the UK Census listed James Coates (Financier) as residing at the 'Mount Royal Hotel' in London. Edith Coates and Veronica Mann (both of private means) were staying at the 'Basil Street Hotel' also in London. On October 7th 1939 all three boarded the 'SS President Harding' at Southampton, bound for New York. Their last address was listed as 6 Grays Inn Square in London.

The ship arrived in New York on October 21st and James Coates (along with other passengers) was hospitalized for injuries (a fractured right arm and contusions) sustained when a giant wave had hit the ship in the Atlantic. He was arrested in hospital on November 3rd at the request of Scotland Yard, but was granted a conditional release when the US Labor Department Board of Review decided that he could be deported. He was expected to depart for Australia in December.

On the evening of December 6th 1939 James Coates was on the gangplank of ‘Mariposa' at Los Angeles with Edith and Veronica, intending to depart. At the request of the Swiss Consul due to a cable warrant from Scotland Yard, James was arrested. The ‘News-Pilot’ (California) of December 7th stated that Edith and Veronica would stay to aid him. He was also wanted by French and Swiss authorities, but he protested that he had been arrested twice in London and freed on the same accusation, and that he was a victim of mistaken identity. His alleged partner in the 1936 swindle was serving five years in a French prison.

Australian newspapers in November 1939 reported upon the New York arrest and noted that Mann's wife was "very sweet and charmingly dressed……and had one of the most magnificent diamonds in her solitaire ring that it was possible to imagine”. I am unable to verify when Edith returned to Australia, but the ‘Herald' (Melbourne) of July 21st 1947 states that James Mann/Coates returned on 'Monterey' in July 1940. When the Swiss extradition failed (they would not pay deportation fees) he returned to his life in Melbourne. In the early 1940s James and Edith Coates were living at 543 Toorak Road, but later in the decade they moved to “an elaborate flat” at 50 Walsh Street South Yarra. In February 1941 James Coates was fined £5 for a traffic infringement in his expensive car when returning from the ‘Bacchus Marsh Races’ on

January 15th. He was reportedly hostile to police, having lost a lot of money at the races. I am unable to trace Veronica Mann after her appearance on the 'Mariposa' gangplank in December 1939, and do not even know if she returned to Australia.

The July 21st 1947 'Herald' article related an unconfirmed story about Mann/Coates once swindling the Prince of Wales (now the Duke or York) of several thousand pounds in a racing swindle. Mann himself allegedly boasted about this, but the NSW Police Commissioner did not believe he ever took the Prince down for anything (else they would have heard from Scotland Yard). Coates was also spoken of as the brains behind forgery of petrol coupons and other wartime rackets in Melbourne and Sydney, and in late 1946 he was fined in Melbourne when detectives raided his flat and seized a loaded automatic pistol. He was described as short and plump with a toothbrush moustache and dapper dress, and was a notorious gambler.

For the last few years prior to 1947 the tide of success had turned against James Coates, and when he was charged with vagrancy his wife said they were living on her income (I cannot find any indication that she actually worked and she was always described as a housewife in electoral rolls). Edith reportedly described him as "a good man" who was always doing good for someone. The 'Sun' (Sydney) on July 27th 1947 said that Mann admitted that throwing money around made him feel happy, and "quite a big shot".

James Coates had been warned off every baccarat school in Melbourne. On Sunday 20th July 1947 his bullet-riddled body was found on a vacant allotment at Windsor in Melbourne. He died on the evening of July 19th and the death record records his surname as Coates even though his parents were correctly named. He had many enemies but the death was thought to be the result of a baccarat feud. Police noted that his hair was scented, there was an expensive cigar in his pocket and his well-manicured fingers clutched at the turf. The funeral was held on Tuesday July 22nd and newspapers reported that only Edith and a few of her friends attended. By 1956 the murder was still unsolved.

Edith Coates remained in the flat at 50 Walsh Street in South Yarra until 1967, still not employed according to electoral rolls. In 1968 she moved in with her brother Alfred Joseph Mason and his wife in Kurilpa Queensland. She now called herself Edith Martha Davies (with no sign of a spouse named Davies). She died at Kurilpa on January 10th 1985, as Davies (with the correct parents recorded).

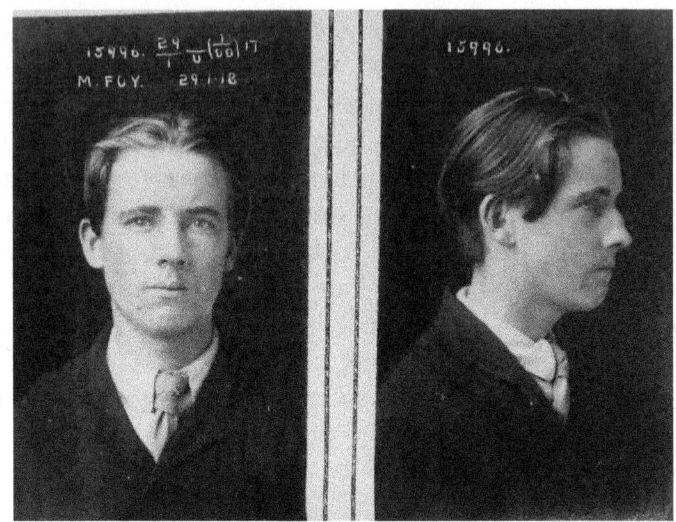

James Mann alias Michael Foy Sydney January 1918

Foy, Michael, *alias* Mann.
Shop-breaker.

VIC Police Gazette 1923

Mann, James, alias Michael Foy.

Bogus landsalesman and confidence man.

(The Customs authorities at Sydney are at present desirous of tracing him for obtaining false passports.)
N.S.W. Photo. Book, 86/133.

July 1929

MRS. E. COATES, of Toorak, Melbourne, looked smart in a grey jersey cloth frock trimmed with white, and a red swathed toque and red belt, when she sailed by the Mariposa yesterday to spend six months in America.

Edith Coates January 1938

James Coates 1939

Edith at funeral July 1947 & grave 2015

Frank H. Powers (1851-1909)

This elusive character spent most of his life as Ross E. Raymond, journalist and reporter. It was only in 1901 that his true identity became publicly known.

Piecing together strands of evidence from newspapers and other records, we find that Frank Powers was born in Pennsylvania in 1851. The identity of his father is not known, but since his uncle-in-law in 1870 was William P. Alcorn of Bucyrus Ohio, his father must have been the son of James Powers (died 1848 in Beaver Pennsylvania) and Ruth Pumphrey (died 1854 in Beaver). Frank's mother was Jane Simpson, born in Pennsylvania in 1827 to William Simpson and Sarah Duncan. Whether she actually married Frank's father or not is unclear.

Frank stated in later life that his father died when he was about the age of five, and that his mother married Barnabus (Bernard) Ford Lee soon after in Poland Ohio. In 1860 in North Beaver, Pennsylvania Jane S. Powers is living with her parents William and Sarah Simpson and her two sons James H. Powers born around 1849 and Frank born around 1852.

After Jane Simpson married widower B.F. Lee in Poland Ohio, three children were born to the couple (Bernard Lyle in 1863, Clyde Duncan in 1866 and Annie). Jane died in Poland Ohio in 1882 and Bernard followed in 1886. Newspapers in 1909 and 1910 reported that Raymond/Powers had gone back to Poland in October 1899 after an absence of more than a quarter of a century, to find his mother had died. He was "deeply affected" when he knelt by her tomb.

On June 22nd 1868 Frank H. Powers enlisted as a midshipman at the Naval Academy in Annapolis Maryland. From October 28th 1869 until November 3rd 1869 he was hospitalized there with cephalalgia (pain in the head). In 1901 he stated that he resigned from the navy on November 4th 1869 because he was demoralized by frequent quarrels with his stepfather who had founded the 'Poland Seminary'. B.F. Lee was allegedly a "strict disciplinarian…. severe and cruel" and Frank became rebellious and wayward. Although he had already resigned by his own account, in June 1870 a newspaper reported that midshipman Frank H. Powers of the US Navy in Annapolis Maryland was visiting his uncle William P. Alcorn in Bucyrus Ohio. This seems to be the last mention of Frank. H. Powers.

By 1872 Frank Powers had morphed into journalist Ross E. Raymond (supposedly born in England) and was working in San Francisco. He reportedly left San Francisco after running into trouble with theatrical manager Thomas Maguire and went to New York. In December 1873 he was arrested for stealing an overcoat at a Fifth Avenue hotel. He gave his name as Arthur J. Holmes. Prison records note that his "wife" Alice was living in San Francisco. On December 31st 1873 he was sent to 'Sing Sing' Prison to serve two years, and he reportedly served the full term. This was said to be his first offense.

The mention of a "wife" in San Francisco indicates to me that Powers/Raymond had already met and was living with Elizabeth Crain. This woman was reportedly devoted to him for more than thirty years before he died. Her father Elisha Crain was in California by 1860 and in San Francisco by 1870. I am unable to find Elizabeth living with her family in California. She may have been older than she admitted (she was older than Frank) or perhaps even married to someone else before she met Ross Raymond?

After his release from 'Sing Sing', Ross Raymond appears as a journalist with the 'Chicago Times' and with the 'American' in Baltimore Maryland from at least January 1877. In March 1879 he was the drama critic for the 'Philadelphia Times'. Newspapers in 1882 reported that Raymond obtained this position by presenting forged letters from Disraeli and others showing he was connected to the 'London Times' and the 'Standard'. He was reportedly dismissed from the 'Philadelphia Times' when his forged recommendations were discovered, although other newspapers suggest that he was dismissed for throwing a young Hebrew of the staff down the office stairs. In Philadelphia he introduced a "large woman" to others as his wife at Brigantine Beach. Later reports that he had married a Californian heiress named Lizzie Linderman in Baltimore are surely false, as was much written about this man.

By early November 1880 Raymond was a New York correspondent for the 'Philadelphia Times' and was also a traveling correspondent for the 'New York Herald'. In the census of 1880 Ross Raymond (reporter) lived with his “wife" Elizabeth in New York. In May 1881 he was able to get his novel ‘No Laggards We' published in New York. By November 1st 1881 he had just resigned from the 'New York Herald' (after a row with the editor Connelly) and become a New York correspondent for the 'London Times'.

In January 1882 Ross Raymond and his wife were traveling around the country and paying their expenses using falsified drafts on the ‘New York Herald'. On Wednesday January 25th he was arrested in New Orleans for swindling and waited in gaol while his wife waited upon a telegraphic money-order to settle the case. This wife was a “fine looking and accomplished lady” and not the “big woman" known as his wife in Philadelphia.

On May 11th 1881 Colorado physician Henry A. Newpher died of pneumonia. His wife Emma (nee Batterson) spent her time in New York, and Ross Raymond became infatuated with her. On August 3rd 1881 as Ross E. Raymond he married Emma S. Newpher in Manhattan. Raymond was described as tall (around 5’10”), jolly, generous, witty, full of fun and well known among women of the world. His tailoring was showy and his sealskin topcoat was of the finest quality. His original “wife" was sadly neglected and surviving in an apartment in Brooklyn New York. In May 1884 Emma S. Raymond wrote to newspapers explaining that she had used Henry Newpher’s life insurance money to release Ross from the New Orleans gaol. In May 1882 the affadavit against

Ross E. Raymond for obtaining money by false pretenses was dismissed in New Orleans.

On March 8th 1882 Ross Raymond was arrested in New York after Julius Chambers (Philadelphia correspondent of the 'New York Herald') accused him of obtaining $100 for traveling expenses by false representations. By March 29th Raymond had been bailed out by "somebody ignorant of the man" who would "have to pay for his absence" since Raymond had jumped his bail and disappeared. Later newspapers state that Messrs. A.M. Palmer and Stephen Fiske had posted bail of $2,000.

By early October 1882 Ross Raymond was in London and working as a reporter for the 'Telegraph'. Emma stated in 1884 that she did not accompany her husband abroad, but went by herself. He apparently deserted her in London when he went to Egypt as a war correspondent. She declared that she had known nothing of his swindling until they reached New Orleans in 1882. In September 1884 she was reported to be supporting herself by singing in a New York casino. I have not been able to determine what happened to Emma S. Batterson/Newpher/Raymond.

Once in England, Ross E. Raymond traveled extensively. On July 26th 1883 as Frank Ross Duncan he sailed on 'Oregon' from England to Canada and swindled money from the Bank of Montreal as a supposed representative of the 'Pall Mall Gazette'. On October 22nd 1883 he arrived in Sydney Australia on the steamer 'City of New York' from San Francisco, and then journeyed to

Melbourne. In December 1883 he was supposedly war correspondent for the London 'Daily News' and was on his way to China. He was sending a series of articles to the Sydney 'Evening News' on lepers of the Sandwich Islands. On February 7th 1884 at Calcutta in India a warrant was issued against him (he was still representing himself as a special correspondent with the London 'Daily News') on a charge of cheating an actress named Verona D'Almain.

In March 1884 as Raymond Bey (an Egyptian notable) Ross Raymond popped up in Paris France after securing a "loan" of 500 francs from a hotelier in Lyons and also leaving his hotel bill unpaid. He was touring through France, borrowing money and living high. He explained the scar on his head as a wound received at the battle of El Teb, when in fact Ross Raymond had acquired the scar when he fell down some stairs in Cincinnati while working for the 'Enquirer' there. He had fought with the son of the newspaper's proprietor and was endeavouring to escape from a thrashing. On March 27th 1884 the US Consul in Leeds England offered a reward for the apprehension of Ross Raymond who was active in England and France. The use of his maternal grandmother's surname Duncan was frequent amongst his aliases. He was described as "a man of good presence, excellent address, unbounded impudence and startling mendacity".

By July 1885 Ross Raymond was believed to be back in America, headquartered at Saratoga and posing as a correspondent of the 'London Standard'. In early October

1885 he was reportedly in Wilmington Delaware (where his wife had supposedly recently been singing in an opera company) after swindling naval officers in Annapolis Maryland as a correspondent for the 'New York Herald'. In March 1886 he disappeared from Detroit where he had been posing as Frank H. Powers (!) and working as a reporter on the 'Tribune'. He had arrived in Detroit supposedly fresh from the Sudan as a representative of the 'London Times'. In April 1886 he paid his bill at the 'Hygeia Hotel' in Old Point Comfort with a worthless draft on the 'Baltimore American'.

On July 29th 1886 Ross Raymond was arrested at the 'Hotel St. George' in New York over a swindle at the 'Belvedere Hotel' in June. On August 17th 1886 at the New York Court of General Sessions this "prince of swindlers" pleaded guilty to the 'Belvedere Hotel' forged cheque and was sentenced to two years in 'Sing Sing'. The prison records indicate that his wife was living in New York, and this was probably Elizabeth Crain.

Ross Raymond was discharged from prison on April 17th 1888 and was taken to Freehold New Jersey to face trial for the passing of a worthless cheque to hotelier Thomas Swift at the Navesink Highlands in the summer of 1886. One report says that the case was compromised and Raymond was released. Another says that Mrs. Raymond interceded for him with New Jersey authorities and he was allowed to pay a small fine. He would now return to England. By late August 1888 he had defrauded the Mayor of Stratford Upon Avon of £100 by pretending to be the nephew of the owner of the 'Philadelphia Ledger'.

On August 19th 1889 Ernest Norton Rolfe (quickly identified as Ross Raymond after a telegram was sent from New York) was arrested at Blackpool in England. As Bennett Burleigh war correspondent in Blackpool he had “dozens of people running after him". He spoke "rather sharply" and had "an extensive vocabulary". In December 1888 he had operated in Birmingham under the name Ritchie, then he swindled (the list is not exhaustive) as Austen Chamberlain (at St. Albans), Major Rhodes of the Royal Dragoons, Captain Reaford, Eric Hastings and Captain Rathburn (at Greenock in Scotland).

While awaiting trial at the Manchester Assizes, Rolfe/Raymond was interviewed on August 23rd 1889 at ‘Preston Gaol'. Even there he wore “a fashionable suit of light grey twill”. Now he was supposedly born in Sydney Australia. On Saturday November 23rd 1889 he faced trial at the Manchester Assizes for defrauding John Harling (confectioner) with a forged bill of exchange for £21 at Blackpool on June 29th 1889, as Bennett Burleigh. He pleaded guilty, and was sentenced to ten years imprisonment. He was tried under Ernest Norton Rolfe, and Ross Raymond was thought to be an alias. For the census of 1891 he is recorded at ‘Portland Prison’ as Ernest Norton Rolfe, journalist, born in Sydney and married.

On April 14th 1898 Ross E. Raymond (born in England with fake parents that listed a mother as Jane Duncan) finally married Elizabeth Crain in Manhattan. In January 1900 he was lodged in prison at Milwaukee Wisconsin as a vagrant pending investigation into a swindle as Major Allenson of the British Army. In the census of June 9th 1900 both Ross E. Raymond (journalist) and wife Elizabeth were living as servants in the household of a musician in Philadelphia Pennsylvania. They had allegedly been married for twenty- four years.

In early March 1901 Raymond was in a New Haven prison for an attempted swindle on the President of Yale University as Lord Rosse of Ireland. On March 26th 1901 he pleaded guilty to grand larceny in the second degree (for a bad draft as James E. Sandys for $200 on the Lincoln National Bank on January 28th). On April 3rd 1901 he was sent to 'Sing Sing' and here he finally admitted his true identity as Frank H. Powers. His wife was living in Keene New Hampshire, and wrote to plead for his release. On April 1st 1901 he was sentenced to four years in prison but with commutation he was released on April 2nd 1904.

For the census of June 1st 1905 Ross E. Raymond (journalist) and wife Elizabeth (housewife) were living in Manhattan New York. In 1870 Elizabeth's youngest sister Velma Crain (an accomplished dressmaker) moved to Carson City Nevada. In 1880 their father Elisha Crain (a farmer) had moved to Carson City, and another married sister lived there also (Elisha died prior to Velma who passed away in 1897). Around 1908 Ross and Elizabeth Raymond moved to Carson City, in the hope that the change of climate would prove beneficial to his failing health. He died on November 24th 1909 after many months of suffering, and was attended on his death-bed by his devoted wife. When asked in an interview why she had clung to him for thirty years, Elizabeth replied that she loved him and believed he was a "grand, big-hearted man of genius". She worked as a dressmaker in Carson City in 1910 but owned her home. She died of cerebral apoplexy on April 4th 1928 and lies in Lone Mountain Cemetery with husband Ross and sister Velma. The death certificate states that she was born on July 12th 1848.

Sketch Ernest Norton Rolfe 1890

Sketch Ross Raymond 1901

Ross Raymond in his prosperous days

Gravestone of Frank Powers' mother Jane Simpson/Powers/Lee

Johann Emil Schlinke (1842-1920)

Schlinke was born in Adelaide South Australia on November 3rd 1842. His parents had emigrated from Germany in search of more religious freedom. When he arrived in January 1839 his father was initially a confectioner, but later he acquired prosperity as a miller. John's mother died when he was ten years old and his father remarried, but he was reportedly quite close to his half-siblings.

Until 1860 John attended St. Peter's Collegiate School. He was captain of the Adelaide Football Club from late 1863, played cricket for the West Norwood Club in the early 1860's and as well as playing the piano he acted as honorary secretary on various committees. In March 1865 he worked as a merchant's clerk and joined the Albert Lodge as a freemason in Adelaide. Until March 1866 Schlinke seemed to be a model citizen. When he became a swindler it was not by design, but through grandiose ambitions and an inability to manage money. He was popular with his family and all who knew him, and was a hard worker throughout his life.

Newspapers on March 13th 1866 reveal that all was not well with young Johann. He had managed to reach Melbourne a few days earlier, and authorities in Adelaide were attempting to stop his departure from there. He had embezzled a considerable sum of money from his employers Francis Clark & Sons. Using the name "J.E. Saunders" Schlinke had already departed on the clipper barque 'Anna' (Captain Watson) bound for San

Francisco in California on March 7th. The debt owed to his employer was around £150 but that was a small proportion of his overall liabilities. The South Australian arrest warrant described Schlinke as around 5’8” in height with light hair. He walked in quick, short steps and wore his hat a little on one side. In his absence, John Emil Schlinke was declared insolvent and creditors seized his assets.

On September 15th 1866 Annie Sophia Schlinke/Salcombe was born in Adelaide. Her mother Kate Maria Salcombe registered John Emil Schlinke as the father. I cannot trace Annie but Kate married a man named John Wilson in Victoria in 1874 and died in East Melbourne as Kate Maria Wilson in November 1886.

Schlinke settled happily in San Francisco, and opened up a book and periodical store. Although “energetic and active in business” he reportedly “led a rather fast life” for someone with his meager financial resources (as he had done in Adelaide). He was “smart, well-educated and plausible” and his dress was “neat and stylish”. The store burned down in May 1867 but insurance covered the loss, and Schlinke then bought an interest in the real estate agency of J.B. Cone. A German emigrant named Christina Dern was renting out furnished rooms in the city from at least 1866, and on July 26th 1867 a girl later known as Liliane Katherine Slinkey was born. On October 13th 1868 Christina Dern married John Emil Schlinke, and Lilian was always treated as their daughter (whether biological or not).

On April 13th 1868 Schlinke appeared in Californian newspapers, having just been arrested at Watsonville after acting as a real estate agent and absconding with $1,630 in coin belonging to a widowed client. His trademark "carbuncle ring" helped authorities to confirm his identity. Mrs. McQuestion got her money back (some courtesy of Cone) and Schlinke was released on bail. In November 1868 the indictment of grand larceny against Schlinke was dismissed because the complaining witness was in San Jose. There were allegations that he had also absconded with $80 belonging to the 'Order of Red Men', held by him as their secretary.

After this lucky escape, John Emil and his new family began using the surname Slinkey. By December 12th 1868 he was advertising as 'J.E. Slinkey & Co. Real Estate and Business Agents' in Market Street San Francisco. Christina still operated furnished rooms, to supplement the family income. On August 11th 1871 Schlinke was naturalized as a citizen of the United States under the name John Emil Slinkey. However, in 1871 in the California Voter Register he was still listed as John Emil Schlinke at 783 Market Street where he and Christina ran furnished rooms.

Late in 1872 John and Christina Slinkey purchased the larger 'Overland House' in Sacramento Street San Francisco, and in early January 1873 they were arraigned before a police court on a charge of assault and battery preferred by one of their boarders. They suggested that the boarder was receiving too many late night male visitors and there was no serious injury, so the case was dismissed. In August 1873 Slinkey was trying to sell his recently renovated property at 783 Market Street, but on September 27th 1873 it burned down (deja vu). Various theories for the origin of the fire included the suggestion that it started in the rear room of Slinkey's lodging house, where a boarder was cooking supper. This time Slinkey estimated that insurance only covered $2,500 of his $4,000 in losses.

On the evening of July 23rd 1874 J.E. Slinkey was arrested for grand larceny in San Francisco. The following day the larceny complaint was dismissed (no details given). He was being sued as a bondsman in June 1874 for improper management of an estate belonging to Luco Jancovich, so perhaps the matters were related? Slinkey was on the committee for the St. George Cricket Club of San Francisco, and playing for the club.

John Emil's commercial star was rising, and on August 16th 1874 he opened the 'Bon Ton Saloon' in the 'California Theatre' building in Bush Street. Early in 1876 he purchased $20,000 of land with improvements in Sausalito, which he ran as the 'Bon Ton Hotel', but he must have overextended himself. In July 1876 he was auctioning off all his holdings and properties to pay creditors. It is likely that his father back in South Australia assisted him financially at this time. When he died in August 1878, Schlinke senior left only £1 sterling in his will to John Emil, who had "received an ample share" during his father's lifetime. Slinkey managed to hang onto 'Overland House' in San Francisco until March 1880, and he slowly rebuilt his assets.

On January 28th 1880 the birth of a daughter to John and Christina Slinkey was notified in newspapers. By the census of June 1880 there was no mention of the child, which probably died in infancy. At this time John Emil was shown as the proprietor of picnic grounds ('Cremorne Gardens') at Martinez in Contra Costa County, which he had purchased in April 1879. His brother Daniel from South Australia (an eccentric "saloon keeper" and later "poundmaster" who had problems with liquor) lived with the family in June 1880. Daniel remained in California until he finally succeeded in overdosing on morphine after several suicide attempts at Sausalito in August 1900.

John Slinkey also leased the bar of the 'Morgan House' at Martinez. When it burned to the ground in April 1881 his insurance again covered his losses. The family left Martinez in early 1882, and on May 1st 1882 John opened the 'El Monte Hotel' (which had been the 'Clifton Hotel') at Sausalito. This was a "first class summer resort". By May 1884 John was acting as secretary for the local 'Society of Old Friends'.

Two more sons were added to the family – Milton Otto Slinkey born May 24th 1882 and Francis Marion Emile Slinkey born August 31st 1883. Family rumours suggest that Milton was in fact the illegitimate son of teenage Lilian, but this was never publicly acknowledged. In newspapers only the christening of Francis was mentioned. Lilian was a talented operatic singer who studied in Milan Italy and taught singing in her own studio in San Francisco. She never married and died as

Slinkey in October 1937. The infant Francis Marion Emile Slinkey died on April 18th 1885. By this time John Emil had graduated from “Captain" to "Colonel" in newspaper articles.

In 1890 Slinkey opened ‘Sausalito Hall’ a “place of amusement". He became owner and manager of the ‘Sausalito News’. In November 1891 he became "financially embarrassed" and turned his property over to five trustees to secure creditors against loss should he fail in business. On July 4th 1893 yet another fire, perhaps caused by fireworks at the 'El Monte Hotel' caused damage to Slinkey's properties in Sausalito.

On July 3rd 1896 one of Slinkey's creditors was suing John Slinkey for his money and wanted the various properties held in trust to be sold. On September 23rd 1896 “Colonel” Slinkey filed for insolvency, owing $50,000 to 122 creditors. From March 1897 his Sausalito assets were sold off. His debts were cleared and in December 1897 he purchased ‘Sausalito House’ (a lodging house at 110 Ellis Street in San Francisco).

On January 13th 1899 Christina Slinkey hung herself in a closet at their Ellis Street lodging house in San Francisco after her husband had gone to bed. John had lost much money of late, an intending purchaser for the Ellis Street property had failed to appear, and she had been in bad health for several years. She was also reportedly disappointed at the failure of Lilian to become a famous singer, after her parents had devoted much of their fortune to her training. Officers and members of the

'Society of Old Friends' attended the funeral. Christina's body was exhumed on January 18th 1899 after an anonymous letter suggested that her death might have been foul play. The letter also accused Slinkey of being involved with another woman. An autopsy had already found the cause of death to be strangulation. Even Christina's brother John Dern believed that it was suicide. John Slinkey was still advertising 110 Ellis Street for sale. The morgue chemist found no trace of poison in Christina's body, and the suicide was upheld.

In March 1899 Slinkey identified by handwriting the author of the anonymous letter. She was said to be Miss/Mrs. May/Mary Lynch, who was purportedly jealous of the Colonel's association with a Mrs. Curtis. Miss/Mrs. Lynch denied the accusation, and nothing came of it.

John Emil Slinkey struggled on in San Francisco, mainly plying real estate. Still catnip to the ladies, on July 1st 1900 his engagement to widow Mrs. J.C. Heitbahn of Chicago Illinois (visiting the coast) was announced. In August 1902 J.E. Slinkey went to Washington "for a vacation". He relocated to Seattle as a real estate agent and married Hattie Heitbahn there on October 9th 1902. He started a branch of the 'Society of Old Friends' there and continued to pose as a 'Colonel'. From 1905 the couple wintered down south in San Francisco. During the summer of 1905 John spent three months in Santa Barbara, capturing and shipping Californian sea lions to Eastern and Europena markets. Hattie visited with friends in Chicago and Milwaukee.

Throughout 1906 (and thus through the earthquake in April) the Slinkeys remained in San Francisco. Milton married there in November 1906 and worked throughout his life as a carpenter (he died in San Francisco in 1953). By December 1906 John had leased a “nice flat" at North Oakland and relocated his real estate business to Oakland.

By May 1907 ‘Colonel’ John Slinkey was living in Goldfield, a mining town in Nevada. In May 1912, as a “real estate man and proprietor of a laundry in Goldfield” he visited Santa Cruz with his wife and thought he might remain there. By February 1913 they had moved back to San Francisco where they lived with Lilian (from 1914 she became Madame Slinkey Durini) and John again managed his Real Estate Syndicate as well as running the ‘Hotel Vincent’ in Turk Street from around 1917. When Hattie departed on extended visits to relatives and friends, he moved back in with Lilian.

On March 4th 1920 Colonel John E. Slinkey died from pneumonia at the ‘Hotel Vincent'. The 'San Francisco Examiner’ explained that he had served in the Confederate Army in the Civil War! He was buried with Christina at the Cypress Lawn Memorial Park. Hattie died in 1922 and was buried in Milwaukee, Wisconsin.

1870s in San Francisco

El Monte Hotel Sausalito at the height of Slinkey's wealth

Lilian

Milton Otto Schlinke late 1880s

George Nicholson Taylor (1843-1932)

Although George served prison time for his embezzlement in Victoria, Australia it may have been his wife Jessie Pearson Dove (nee Cairncross) who orchestrated the situation. She managed to escape punishment, leaving George to take the rap, but she was possibly the charlatan rather than he.

George Nicholson Taylor was born in Jamaica in 1843 and baptized there on April 19th 1844. His father Henry was a missionary to Jamaica from around 1838. He had married Mary Ann Burslem in Lancashire England in 1828. Daughter Mary was baptized in Jamaica in February 1840 and another son Frederick Lessing was baptized in October 1844. By 1851 the family were living in Wednesbury Staffordshire. Reverend Henry Taylor died in May 1884 in Bradford Yorkshire and his wife Mary Ann (nee Burslem) died in December 1863. Both lie in Utley Cemetery in West Yorkshire.

In 1861 George Nicholson Taylor was still living with his family (who were prosperous enough to employ a domestic servant) in Keighley Yorkshire and his occupation was "seaman". His Victorian prison record reveals that he left Liverpool and arrived in Melbourne (probably as crew) in 1862. The name of the ship is indecipherable.

In late 1863 George Nicholson Taylor married Jessie Pearson Dove Cairncross in Melbourne. In September of that year the still unmarried Jessie was a schoolmistress in Williamstown. In the 1841 UK census the Cairncross family were living in Northumberland England and Jessie's father William Hay Cairncross is shown as an "engineer". In 1851 Davina Cairncross (nee Dove) was widowed and living with her two children (Jessie and William McGregor) in Liverpool. She was listed as a "housekeeper" and had one lodger with her. The family arrived in Melbourne on 'Neptune' on September 1st 1853. By 1856 Davina seems to have been running a shop in South Melbourne and by 1862 she was living at 15 Cecil Street in Williamstown and letting "genteel apartments". Jessie's brother William McGregor Cairncross became a storekeeper at Williamstown and was appointed comptroller of stores in the Defence Department . He died in 1903 and Davina Cairncross (nee Dove) died in April 1890.

From 1864 until 1866 George Nicholson Taylor lived in property at Williamstown owned by Jessie's uncle Alexander James Dove. From 1867 George moved between Footscray and Williamstown and worked as a clerk. Although some researchers state that George's work as a clerk and then accountant was the result of Jessie's prompting, his brother Frederick Lessing Taylor was an accountant's apprentice and bookkeeper in Lancashire by 1861.

In August 1879 George Nicholson Taylor was acting manager for the 'Land Credit Bank of Australasia' that had been incorporated in 1876. He and his family were living in Albert Street Footscray. In January 1880 the funeral of Jessie's aunt Eliza Trail Craigie Beynon (nee

Dove) left from the Taylor residence in Albert Street. George still did not own his own property. In 1881 the family moved to Prahran and in 1882 and 1885 Jessie Pearson Dove Taylor is shown as the owner of the family residence in Denbigh Road Prahran. In November 1889 Jessie is also the owner of son Henry William Burslem's residence 'Tucson' 36 High Street West Prahran/Windsor and her mother Davina Cairncross's residence next door at 38 High Street.

Jessie bought up real estate with abandon (she reportedly worked as a milliner in the early years of her marriage and was a keen businesswoman). No doubt her husband's access to money as manager of the 'Land Credit Bank' led both of them to live beyond their means. In 1884 George (without the knowledge of the directors) had established a current account with the bank and by August 14th he was overdrawn by £2,272 3s 10d. On July 31st 1884 a promissory note for £1,290 2s 6d was paid to the bank and in August he transferred it into his own account and reduced his overdraft. In late 1886 or in 1887 the Taylors purchased a mansion 'Bonnington' at 25 High Street West Prahran/Windsor from previous owner Richard McDonnell.

In March 1891 George Nicholson Taylor was ingeniously manipulating money between his own account and Jessie's account at the bank to avoid the detection of their overdrafts. To balance the books he deposited a promissory note for £5,303 8s 8d to the bank in Jessie's name. In late November 1891 George knew he would have to meet with directors of the 'Commercial Bank' about problems with the 'Land Credit Bank' and was about to be discovered. Taking £14,728 from his own account (now in overdraft by £52,000) he paid it into Jessie's account (now in credit) and drew two cheques for £1,942 and £5,303 to retire promissory notes belonging to himself and his wife. The machinations were described as a "series of mercantile frauds as extraordinary as any ever brought to light in the colony".

Apart from her real estate expenses, Jessie Taylor had underwritten the formation of the 'Hansom Cab Publishing Company' run by Frederick Trischler in 1887 for the express purpose of publishing the book 'Mystery of a Hansom Cab' written by Fergus Hume. She had purchased the copyright to the book from Hume for a paltry sum in August 1887. The book sold well and was even published by the company in London, but Hume quarreled with Trischler and by January 1890 the 'Hansom Cab Publishing Company' was defunct. Presumably Jessie did not then receive royalties from the book sales (it was published by another company in New York in 1888).

On December 2nd 1891 the 'Land Credit Bank of Australasia' closed its doors owing £100,000 to depositors and £50,000 to bankers and public works. George blamed a recent "stupid run" on withdrawals precipitated by the closing of the 'City of Melbourne Building Society'. On Monday night December 14th depositors and shareholders met and discovered that the losses were largely due to the "excessive overdrafts of the manager" amounting to over £60,000. George, Jessie and eldest son Henry had overdrafts totaling £114,000 that were offset by securities of £11,000 and a bill of exchange for £43,590 drawn by Jessie on April 22nd (after the overdrafts were discovered) and payable within six months. Taylor was already suspended and there were calls for his arrest. The bank would be wound up.

On the evening of December 15th 1891 George Nicholson Taylor was arrested at his residence. The charge was that "between July 15th 1889 and April 11th 1891, being then manager of the Land Credit Bank of Australasia Limited, he defrauded the said bank by omitting a material particular in the books of account in which the weekly balances of the individual accounts were shown". He was described as a regular church-goer and "exceptionally religious" Presbyterian. While Jessie had property valued between £50,000 and £60,000 George had indulged in land speculation at Malvern and Coburg since 1887. He still owed £72,000 on these but the equity had been seized as security back in April when his large overdraft was discovered.

While eldest son Henry William Burslem Taylor was attempting to find bail (and failing) George languished in Melbourne Gaol. On December 11th 1891 Jessie had signed a contract for sale on 'Bonnington' at 25 High Street to an electrician for £3,000. The property was held by the 'Land Credit Bank' as security for Jessie's bill of exchange. Since the 'Land Credit Bank' closed its doors she had reportedly barricaded herself inside the house with her daughters citing illness and set her dogs loose on anyone attempting to enter. On December 12th she sailed for Auckland as Mrs. Pearson with the two youngest daughters Georgina and Annie.

On December 22nd 1891 the purchaser of 'Bonnington' paid Henry William Burslem Taylor £3,000 in cash and took possession of the property. Henry paid solicitor John Hopkins £500 to represent his father in court. He gave George Meldrum Henderson £1,900 to pass to his sister Margaret Haldane, an old family friend. This was supposedly to be kept in trust for the remaining three daughters in Melbourne. Mrs. Haldane banked it in her own name on December 23rd 1891 and Henderson left for Auckland under the surname Meldrum that day. Henderson testified that he met Jessie in Auckland and we must surmise that he passed the remaining £600 from the house sale to her there.

On January 5th 1892 William McGregor Taylor (second son) attempted to withdraw the £1,900 on behalf of Mrs. Haldane but the bank refused to cash her cheque because the 'Land Credit Bank' had a writ of attachment against her. While Hopkins, Henderson and Haldane were considered to have participated in assisting Jessie to get away and making shady transactions, in late February 1892 the court accepted that the electrician had properly purchased 'Bonnington' and its contents and the writ of attachment against him was dismissed. From early March 1892 the two-story mansion on the corner of High and Donald Streets plus oil paintings, drawings, costly furnishings and two pianofortes was up for sale. In February 1893 it was a "superior" boarding house.

At 'Melbourne Supreme Court' on February 26th 1892 George Nicholson Taylor was found by a jury to be guilty on two charges of fraud as manager of a body corporate relating to stealing promissory notes (£1,290 2s 6d and £5,303 8s 8d as described above). On March 1st 1892 he was sentenced to two years imprisonment with hard labour.

On Friday July 29th 1892 George Nicholson Taylor was further found guilty of defrauding the 'Land Credit Bank' of £37,000 in conspiracy with a customer named Charles Ernest Clarke from 1882 until the suspension of the bank. On July 30th Taylor was fined £5,000 (to be levied on his property only) and sentenced to a further eight years in prison. Justice Hood remarked that he had been "bitten by the gambling mania". George moaned that all his gains had gone into land companies, in some of which bank directors had been "mixed up". The convictions were reaffirmed upon appeal in September 1892.

We leave George languishing in 'Pentridge' to follow the rest of the family. In January 1892 Jessie, Georgina and Annie left Auckland for San Francisco. The eldest daughters Devina, Jessie and Jane were staying with Margaret Haldane in South Yarra. Henry William Burslem Taylor's wife gave birth to a son in late February 1892 and it is likely that his family left for San Francisco soon after. By 1893 one Samuel Greenberg was living at their address in 36 High Street Prahran.

By 1894 Henry W.B. Taylor was living in Oakland California and working as a bookkeeper for 'Marcus &

Remmel'. His mother lived at another address in Oakland and had returned to dressmaking. By 1895 the rest of the family had arrived in Oakland and lived at 1828 Eagle Avenue. On Saturday March 20th 1899 George was released from 'Pentridge' early owing to good conduct and Jubilee remissions. He was immediately re-arrested for non-payment of the £5,000 fine and taken to 'Melbourne Gaol'. It was doubtful that he had sufficient property to liquidate the debt, and possibly faced indefinite detention until the fine was paid. George stated that his eldest son Henry supported the family (in fact all the children had jobs as clerks, saleswomen and bookkeepers in Oakland). His wife had unsuccessfully tried to make a living by dressmaking and keeping a boardinghouse. On July 5th 1899 the Attorney General decided to believe George and he was finally set free.

From this point on George Nicholson Taylor took on the name George Lawton Taylor (I cannot find any family reference or other reason for the Lawton). He departed Sydney for San Francisco as G. Lawton Taylor on 'SS Mariposa' on August 30th 1899 and arrived on September 22nd. For the USA census of 1900 the whole family were living together at 2009 Pacific Avenue in Alameda California. George was restored as the head of the household and was listed as a "speculator". Henry had qualified to practise as an attorney in December 1898, and he and his wife and two children are living in the household as well. Only Jessie senior and Jane have no listed occupations.

Henry and family moved to San Francisco, while George moved to 2101 Clement Avenue in Oakland California and worked as a bookkeeper and accountant and dabbled in real estate. Devina married in 1902, Jessie in 1903, and Georgina in 1904 before George and his wife appear to have left Oakland for a time. When Annie married in Alameda in 1907 Henry gave the bride away. In 1909 George was living with Henry in San Francisco and working as a bookkeeper, but I cannot find him in the census of 1910.

By 1912 George was back as an accountant living in Oakland at 1910 24th Avenue. Jessie Pearson Dove Taylor (nee Cairncross) died of pneumonia at the "family home" in Oakland in January 1919, leaving behind a "devoted husband". By this time Henry was Mayor of San Anselmo and President of the Board of Health there. In 1920 George lived with Henry and family in San Anselmo and was a "retired broker". In 1930 he lived with Devina and her husband in Oakland. On June 18th 1932 George L. Taylor a "beloved father" and a "native of Port Royal Jamaica" died in Oakland.

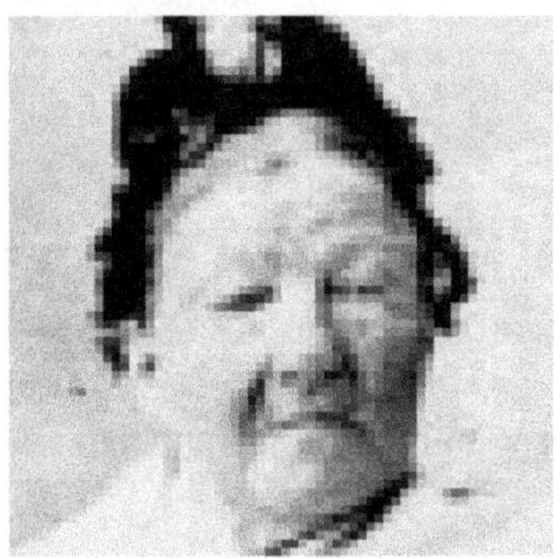

Jessie Pearson Dove Cairncross

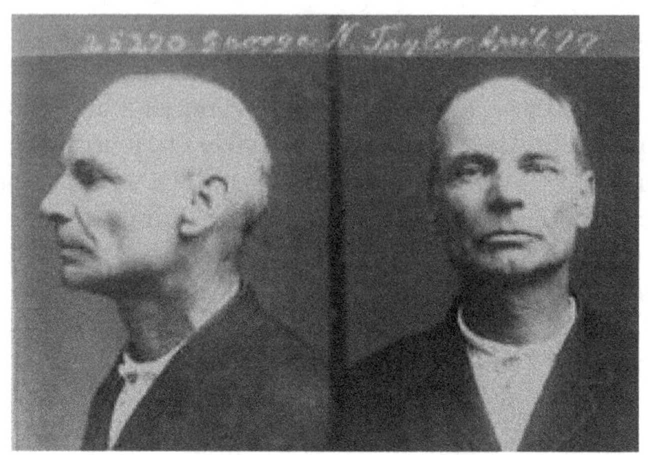

George Nicholson Taylor 1899 Victoria

Henry William Burslem Taylor

www.ingramcontent.com/pod-product-compliance
Lightning Source LLC
LaVergne TN
LVHW010547160826
845677LV00013B/3036

* 9 7 9 8 3 5 3 2 4 4 8 9 9 *